GROUP LEADER TRAINING

A Biblical Manual for Small Group Leaders and Teachers in the Local Church

By

Adam Erlichman

With

"Most churches cite a lack of leadership as one of their most pressing challenges. And while all have some leadership development processes, most are not formalized, methodical, and repeatable processes that consistently equip and produce leaders. The Group Leader Training Course Workbook is designed to help fill that gap. Adam has done a masterful job of distilling key group leadership principles into a framework that is universal enough for churches to use out of the box – and flexible enough to be easily customized as desired. If you are tired of scrambling for leadership, this resource is for you!"

– **JUSTIN FRAZIER**

Executive Pastor, Discipleship at Cottonwood Creek Church

Adam thoughtfully lays out a thorough yet simple how-to-guide for new and experienced leaders alike who desire to lead small groups in the local church. This work is theologically strong and thoughtfully practical. It discusses a successful method for leading groups that has been tested time and time again with great success. I highly recommend this book to anyone leading in the local church at any level.

– **PAUL PEARSON**

Small Group Leader & Sunday School Teacher

We were able to reap the benefit directly of the teachings in Adam's book. This book lays out how to develop and recognize healthy groups, and how to move them to be more involved in the needs of the church. We personally experienced this with our group and had other groups start out from what we learned in our group. This is a must have book for groups!

– **KATE MAJOR**

Small Group Leader & Coach

Adam has put together a great resource for group leadership training. Having a ready-to-go resource that helps prospective leaders evaluate their call to leadership and equips them with group leadership essentials will be a very useful tool for many churches. Adam has done the heavy lifting, and church leaders get the benefit of quality training without the hours spent to develop it.

– **PHIL TODD**

Spiritual Formations Ministries Team Leader at the Southern Baptists of Texas Convention, 30+ years of experience as Executive, Small Groups, and Student Pastor

"There are many small group books written for staff. This one is for the small group leader! Adam has developed a holistic resource (head, heart, and hands) to multiply top-quality group leaders. If you want to grow your groups (quality and quantity), you need this leadership training curriculum."

– **STEVE GLADEN**

Pastor of Small Groups at Saddleback Church, Lake Forest, CA, Author of ***Small Groups with Purpose, Leading Small Groups with Purpose***, and ***Planning Small Groups with Purpose***, and founder of the Small Group Network

The old saying is 'when you know who you are, you know what to do.' For group leaders, this book will tell you what you should be so that you will know what to do when leading your group. Biblically accurate and scalable for training up group leaders.

– **DUSTIN FLUECKIGER**

Married Community Director at Watermark Community Church Dallas, TX

This masterpiece put together by Adam Erlichman is a great resource for any small group pastor, leader, and anyone considering leading a small group in a local church. Adam does an amazing job of presenting practical ways to biblically lead groups in the local church. I see this as an excellent resource specifically for those who are looking to start a small group ministry and are looking for a biblical model of how to get started. I highly recommend this book and personally plan on giving it to my own small group leadership team.

– **MATT MOORE**

Pastor of Groups and Connections at Providence Church, Frisco, TX, Small Group Network Dallas Director

Community is forged, not found. What a profound truth that helps guide the goals of small group. Adam's passion for transformation is on display as he guides readers through 5 essential components of healthy small groups. GLT is both philosophical and practical. Challenging yet approachable. It's a true gift to me and will be an ongoing asset as I train our group leaders.

– **TYLER DOWNING**

Next Steps & Small Group Pastor at Gospel City Church Granger, IN

This book combines biblical clarity with hard-earned pastoral wisdom. The emphasis on moving people toward maturity in Christ with stages that are easy to identify is particularly helpful. I recommend it wholeheartedly.

– **BRUCE GARNER**

Lead Pastor at Crosspoint Church Huntington Beach, CA, Author of *The Resilient Pastor: How to Remain Effective and Finish Well in Ministry*

Copyright © 2021 by Build Groups, LLC
All rights reserved.
Printed in the United States of America

ISBN: 9798462560194

Published by Build Groups, LLC in Pilot Point, Texas.
For more books by Build Groups, visit us at:
www.buildgroups.net/resources

Editor: Lindsay Cummings
Cover design: Russell Wofford
Interior design: Farhan Shahid

Scripture quotations are from The ESV® Bible
(The Holy Bible, English Standard Version®)
Copyright © 2001 by Crossway, a publishing ministry of Good News Publishers.
2011 Text Edition. All rights reserved.

FOREWARD

I am happy to commend this book to anyone wanting to grow their group ministry. I have watched as Adam has successfully equipped men and women for groups ministry through the group leader training course. Each chapter contains tried and proven training that equips and prepares leaders for successful group leadership.

Many churches have attempted groups ministry over the years only to achieve lackluster results. Group leaders and group members experience frustration when their group fails to thrive according to the prescribed "method," and the effort is soon abandoned. Based on past failures, when someone brings up the need for groups ministry, the response usually goes like this: "We've tried groups here before, and they will never work at our church."

I admit that I have fallen prey to the quick fix mentality for the successful development of groups ministry. I have spent hours and dollars reading groups ministry books, listening to podcasts, and attending conferences. Always elusive, the perfect plug-and-play program that meets the requirements of lead pastors or elder boards always feels just out of reach or right around the next corner. But let's face it, there is no program that is truly transmittable from the context of one ministry to the next. There is no programmatic silver bullet for group ministry success.

There is a biblical solution though – leadership development.

Based on the biblical principles of discipleship, leadership development aims at fostering the gifts of the Holy Spirit in God's people and equipping them for ministry. This is not a quick fix; if that is what you're looking for, you won't find it here. What you will find is a manual for leadership development that is focused on the long game.

Leadership development is the one activity in the church that allows ministry leaders to extend themselves and do more with less effort effectively. Developing leaders takes time and investment; however, the results can lead to transformative ministry.

I have watched with great satisfaction as the leadership training in this book has been implemented successfully at Midway Church. Time and again, men and women have committed to being trained as godly leaders. Consequently, we have seen the development of individuals who are more Christ-like, families that are growing in their faith, and strong groups that are doing life together.

Whether you are starting or strengthening your groups ministry, the recipe for success isn't in programs, it's in leadership development.

- **TODD WITTE**

  Executive Pastor, Midway Church

  Former Director of North Texas Baptist Bible Fellowship

  Adjunct Professor, Baptist Bible College in Springfield, MO

ACKNOWLEDGEMENTS

First and foremost, this book is dedicated to my wife, Anna. Late nights of leading many new group leader trainings over the years, you have selflessly and sacrificially served our family in wrestling three wild boys to bed those evenings. You are a true miracle worker of love, grace, and gentleness in their lives and mine. None of this is possible without you, my beloved.

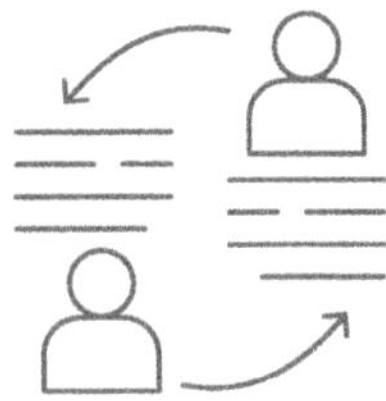

Second, I dedicate this book to the countless group leaders who gave of their time, energy, and resources to becoming all God made them to be for the sake of many group members they now lead. My mentor, friend, and pastor, Jeff Scott, always said in my early formative years . . .

"I learn more from you, than you do from me."

"I learn more from you, than you do from me." Oh, how true his familiar statement is. Group Leaders, you sharpen me more than I sharpen you. Praise God for your hearts to see spiritual transformation in the souls of many families, friends, coworkers, and enemies. As another mentor of mine has said . . . .

Group Leaders, You are my heroes.

– JARED MUSGROVE

GROUP LEADER TRAINING

A Biblical Manual for Small Group Leaders and Teachers in the Local Church

By

Adam Erlichman

With

build groups | one another together

Dallas, Texas

OVERVIEW

Group leader training at www.buildgroups.net/glt

Training Descriptions

ASSESSMENT

Create a free member account on www.buildgroups.net and download the GLT Assessment to fill out and send to your pastor/trainer to help them assess strengths and weaknesses to tailor the training to your specific needs.

GLT 01	**HEALTHY GROUPS** The first training discusses what a Healthy Group is and is not. We also talk about what bearing the Gospel has on a healthy group.
GLT 02	**FELLOWSHIP** The second training explores how a group fellowships with God and one another. Tools on how to help a group fellowship are provided.
GLT 03	**GROW** The third training examines how you can intentionally help disciples grow in groups. Growth assessment tools are provided.
GLT 04	**SERVE** The fourth training equips you to see the role you play in mobilizing a group from consuming to contributing.
GLT 05	**MULTIPLY** The fifth and final training shows how a group can role model sharing and spreading the gospel far and wide through group multiplication and witnessing to unbelievers.

The Process Overview

ASSESSMENT

Request a GLT Assessment from www.buildgroups.net/glt to fill out and send to your pastor/trainer, which helps them assess strengths and weaknesses to tailor the training to your specific needs.

GLT 01

HEALTHY GROUPS

- Video Training & Fill-in-the-Blanks
  8 MINUTES
- Essential Belief Assessment
  10 MINUTES
- Group Discussion Training
  2 HOURS

GLT 02

CONNECT

- Video Training & Fill-in-the-Blanks
  10 MINUTES
- Essential Belief Assessment
  9 MINUTES
- Group Discussion Training
  2 HOURS

GLT 03

GROW

- Video Training & Fill-in-the-Blanks
  11 MINUTES
- Essential Belief Assessment
  7 MINUTES
- Group Discussion Training
  2 HOURS

GLT 04

SERVE

- Video Training & Fill-in-the-Blanks
  11 MINUTES
- Essential Belief Assessment
  10 MINUTES
- Group Discussion Training
  2 HOURS

GLT 05

MULTIPLY

- Video Training & Fill-in-the-Blanks 11 MINUTES
- Essential Belief Assessment 13 MINUTES
- Group Discussion Training 2 HOURS

The Group Leader Training Course is designed to offer a holistic training process that can be facilitated in any local church.
Learn more at www.buildgroups.net/glt

QR Code Instructions

Pull up your phone's camera, hold over the QR code above, wait for a notification link to pop down from the top of your screen, click it, and it will take you to the website.

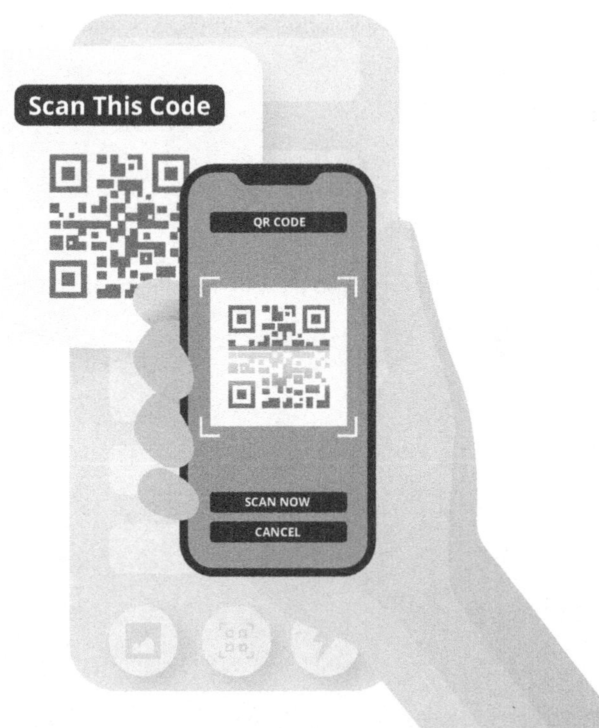

INTRODUCTION

For six years, the Lord has gifted me beautiful and brutal moments in ministry that have compiled the contents of the Group Leader Training Course: workbook, leader assessments, videos, fill in the blank, doctrinal assessments, and more. Great apprehension has arisen within me every time I have contemplated publishing this training. I have felt fear, worry, and anxiety over the completion of this for a multitude of differing reasons. It was only recently I realized why I felt these ways. The Group Leader Training represents thousands of people. Group leaders, Sunday School teachers, members of each, and unbelievers yet to encounter Christ's gospel. Their stories with one another and how the gospel radically altered their lives. I recount the many lives eternally affected by men, women, and teenagers who went through the Group Leader Training and how God instrumentally used them in other people's lives. Overwhelming doesn't begin to express my feelings of these experiences. A devastating gratefulness wrecks my typical calm composure. I feel immensely blessed to play a small part in seeing the power of Christ radically change people's stories forever. The source of my apprehension can be summed up in two verses:

"For God is my witness, how I yearn for you all with the affections of Christ Jesus.

– **PHILIPPIANS 1:8**

My little children, for whom I am again in the anguish of childbirth until Christ is formed in you!

– **GALATIANS 4:19**

I could tell you about two group leaders, Matt and Amy, who loved on David and Kristina as the lone and only couple that attended the group for the entire semester. As a result, they were saved, and Matt had the privilege of baptizing both.

Another married couple, Sam and Grace, became group leaders. Sam said he would go through the Group Leader Training but would probably never lead a group. Years later, they have seen several people give their lives to Christ, begin to serve, and much of the group go through the Group Leader Training course themselves to start their own groups. Not only do Sam and Grace lead a group, but now they coach other group leaders.

On the other hand, many current and former pastors have gone through the Group Leader Training process and found great value in it. Despite decades of pastoral experience from some of these individuals, they had something to take away from the training as well.

Sitting in Chick Fil A, I was privileged to lead Dusty, husband and father of three daughters, to receive Christ as his Lord and Savior. Soon after, I baptized this large, bearded countryman. Almost immediately, he and his wife joined a group, and he began learning everything he could. He was hungry to believe bigger, follow faithfully, and know God more. Nearly a year later, he began serving and contributing. As I write these words, two and a half years later, he and his wife have completed the Group Leader Training and begun co-leading in a group.

It is my conviction that as the local church builds leaders, groups will be started. As new groups are started, disciples will be made. Purposefully, I firmly believe this is the model Jesus left us to turn the world upside down and fulfill the Great Commission. Jesus chose twelve disciples for his group. He poured into them for three years so that they would in turn pour themselves out for many other disciples to be made. Here is the root of the repeated phrase throughout this book

"Build Leaders.
Build Groups.
Build Disciples."

My three primary aims in writing this book are:

01	*Provide doctrinally deep content married to accurate application*
02	*Scripturally precise content that drives and explains the why behind essential and best practices.*
03	*Simple, full, and considerate content of everyday church lay leaders.*

No matter who you are, where you are, what you've done in ministry, how much or little you know, the Group Leader Training course is for you. It has equipped, inspired, challenged, taught, corrected, and ministered to the souls of many men and women.

Leading groups is far too important to leave up to chance or wishful thinking that group leaders may just figure it out along the way without any training or equipping. Truly, as my personal mentor, Jared Musgrove, has so passionately and genuinely said:

You are my heroes. Group Leaders are the front lines of spiritual formation. You are the front line. You are my heroes.

Likewise, his statement echoes true to the beat of my heart. It is my hope that this resource, paired with the training, will equip, sharpen, and move you to see how God can use you. Whether you are nervous or excited about this endeavor, let me encourage you with this: you can do anything God wants you to. Let's explore this journey together of what God is calling you to. It may be bigger than what you've ever imagined before. I pray that is the case.

With the utmost love, affection, and jealousy for you to be vessels of God's transforming power to others,

– **ADAM ERLICHMAN**

Table of
CONTENTS

HOW TO BEST USE THIS BOOK

Through the years, this course primarily helped potential new group leaders explore a call to possibly serve as a group leader. However, it became very clear that potential new group leaders and veteran group leaders profited from this training. It helped clarify, focus, and equip them to do the work of ministry through groups. Therefore, there are several methods of using this book. One size does not fit all. The Group Leader Training course is not a silver bullet that perfectly prepares and propels group leaders into great gospel Christlike leadership. However, it has and can better position many more group leaders far and wide to make disciples.

Here's how to best use this book

01 Use this as a manual to reference, not information to memorize.

02 Watch the video, fill in the blank, and essential belief affirmations at the start of each chapter.

03 Discuss the training questions in a group setting. Experiencing these truths by practicing and modeling versus knowing about them is monumentally different.

04 If any of this is different or disagrees with the Groups philosophy of your local church, submit to and go with their way over this – Unity is more effective than best practices.

A NOTE TO POTENTIAL NEW LEADERS

Through the years, the contents of this book have aided many potential new group leaders to ***explore*** where God was calling them to serve. As opposed to solely preparing one to be a group leader, the group leader training course has more so been used to help people discern whether God was calling them to be a group leader or not. From beginning to end, this is an open hands process of exploring what God is calling an individual to in ministry service. The majority of people who go through this training discover that they are being called to lead a group; however, there are many who do not end up becoming a group leader. Worst case scenario, if leading a group isn't what God is calling you to, you will be more than equipped to be a healthy, supportive, and encouraging group member. Group leaders would beg for a faithfully equipped group member like you in their group. You are more valuable than you know. If you discover God is calling you to be a group leader, this material will equip you with a meaningful understanding of Biblical community and instruct you on how to build it with one another in a Group.

"The best leadership is that which is acquired, not that which is sired (born into)."

– **CHARLES H. SPURGEON**

A NOTE TO EXISTING GROUP LEADERS

Through the years, the contents of this book have been used to train potential new group leaders to explore a possible call to serve as a group leader. However, many long term group leaders and pastors who have gone through this training claim it is the best training they've ever seen on leading groups. Whether you are seeking to start or strengthen yourself as a group leader, I am confident that you will find worthwhile information in this book and training. No matter if you have led a group for years, decades, or months, you will find some wonderful Biblical truths that shape how you lead a group. Much of the training will serve as reminders of truths you knew previously. However, you may connect them in a different light or even be refreshed. Nonetheless, I challenge you to dive into the Group Leader Training course to consider why, what, and how you do what you do as a group.

"Give me six hours to chop down a tree and I will spend the first four sharpening the axe."

– **ABRAHAM LINCOLN**

GROUP LEADER TRAINING

HEALTHY GROUPS

01

OBJECTIVES

Define what a healthy group is and is not. Discern what practices, qualities, expectations, and purposes constitute a healthy group.

SCRIPTURE READING

Acts 2:42-47

TRAINING #1 CHECKLIST

- o Video
- o Fill-in-the-Blanks
- o Essential Belief Assessment
- o Group Discussion
- o Read Chapter 1

CHECKLIST 01

VIDEO

Instructions

Prior to reading the following chapter and attending your next training . . .

Go to www.buildgroups.net/glt1 and create your free membership account.

Login, watch the video, and fill-in-the-blanks on the following page.

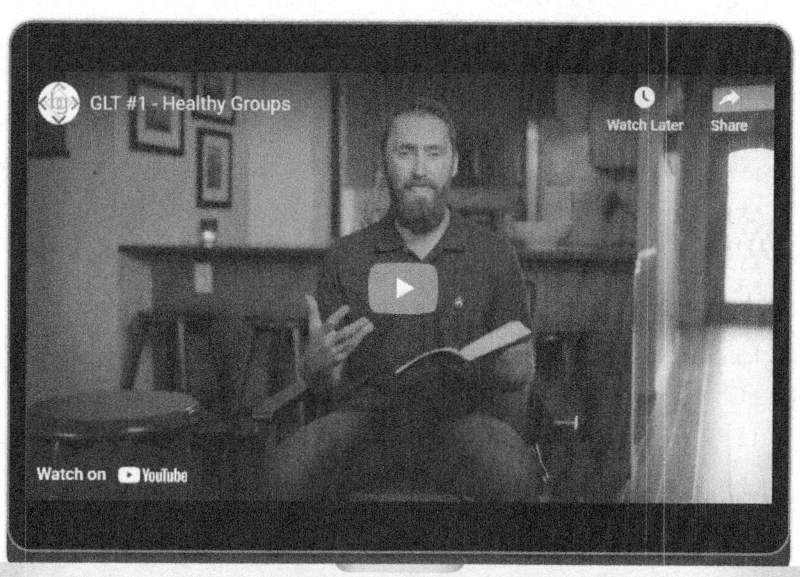

CHECKLIST 02

FILL IN THE BLANKS

An overview of each training session can be seen at the beginning of each training session chapter.

This is an opportunity for you to _________ a potential call to be a group leader.

> *But you are a chosen race, a royal priesthood, a holy nation, a people for hi sown possession, that you may proclaim the excellencies of him who called you out of darkness into his marvelous light. Once you were not a people, but now you are God's people; once you had not received mercy, but now you have received mercy.*
>
> – **1 PETER 2:9-10**
>
> Read Acts 2:42-47

This passage is the bedrock passage for what it means to be the church and how to be a healthy group.

1. The ______________ of God are being proclaimed through the establishment of the church.

2. The change is they have now been empowered with the same power that raised Christ from the dead, ___________ ___________.

3. You may feel ___________ about starting this Group Leader Training

The wrong question: "Do I want to be a group leader?"

The right question: "Does God want me to be a group leader?"

4. You can do _________ God wants you to do.

5. My final encouragement to you: do not put your confidence in your ____________ or lack of ____________.

6. Whether you don't have the ______________, skill set, or speaking ability.

7. Put your _______________ in what God can do in you and through you.

8. God may have a bigger ________ for you than you even do for yourself.

CHECKLIST 03

ESSENTIAL BELIEF ASSESSMENT

Purpose

To expose and give people the opportunity to explore the essential beliefs or doctrines of the Christian faith. This is not a pass or fail exam; but, rather, it is a chance to learn important Biblical beliefs together.

		True	False	Unsure
01	God is a perfect being and cannot make a mistake.	☐	☐	☐
02	There is one true God in three persons: God the Father, God the Son, and God the Holy Spirit.	☐	☐	☐
03	The Gospel is that Jesus Christ died a literal death on a cross for the sins of the world.	☐	☐	☐
04	God is unconcerned with my day-to-day decisions.	☐	☐	☐
05	Only those who trust in Jesus Christ alone as their Savior receive God's free gift of eternal salvation.	☐	☐	☐
06	The Bible has the authority to tell us what we must do.	☐	☐	☐
07	Before God, humanity is of the same value, worth, and dignity as animals.	☐	☐	☐
08	Everyone sins a little, but most people are good by nature.	☐	☐	☐
09	God created humanity because he was lonely.	☐	☐	☐
10	God accepts the worship of all religions, including Christianity, Judaism, and Islam.	☐	☐	☐

Refer to this link for the answer guide: https://www.buildgroups.net/eba1

CHECKLIST 04

GROUP DISCUSSION

1. Introductions

    - Name
    - Family
    - What you do for work?
    - What group are you in?
    - How long have you been at this church?
    - What is your ministry/volunteer background?
    - Where do you desire to possibly lead?

2. What were your thoughts on the video?

3. Read and discuss Acts 2:42-47. What sticks out to you? Looks important? Seems significant?

4. You have 90 minutes for the group gathering. How would you divvy up time between Fellowship, Study, and Prayer? Why?

5. Go around in a circle one by one. What is one quality of a healthy group?

CHECKLIST 05

HEALTHY GROUPS

Healthy Groups, Healthy Leaders

Healthy groups must start with ***Healthy Leaders.*** Groups absent of healthy leaders will be very difficult, if not impossible, to see a healthy group formed.

Fortunately, the Bible doesn't leave open ended what a healthy leader is made up of. The Apostle Paul wrote to Timothy and Titus about the necessary qualities of a healthy leader. Better yet, the ***Healthy Leader*** qualities listed by the Apostle Paul are 90% character and have little to do with skill or ability. Therefore, it is important to recognize that healthy groups do not require a ***Gifted Leader***, but they do necessitate a ***Godly one.*** On the other end of the spectrum, a healthy group does not demand a ***Perfect Leader***, but one desiring ***Progress.*** So be encouraged, because anyone could be a leader, but not everyone should.

In summary, a Healthy Group requires a Healthy Leader who is ***godly, imperfect,*** in ***desire of progress***, and ***may or may not*** have extraordinary gifts to lead.

CHARACTER

It is important to note that being a healthy leader is not a prerequisite to taking the Group Leader Training. Are pre-existing character qualities helpful? Yes, absolutely. However, at the beginning, it is not necessary to feel like all of them are met. Focus most on ***Movement*** and ***Progress*** towards these Christlike characteristics. What ***trajectory*** for godliness does a person possess? If the choice is between a skilled, stagnate leader with experience and a potential new leader with a high trajectory for godliness, ***trajectory*** is the preferred option. By trajectory, it is not so much about instant progress as it is desire. Trajectory has more to do with hunger than any actual result. Over time, a high hunger for godliness leads to these godly character qualities being formed.

COMPETENCY

Another important matter to consider. What competencies are present? There are no prerequisites of skill, competency, or gifting that must precede commencing the Group Leader Training. In fact, no skills present is acceptable. The purpose of the Group Leader Training is to help equip a person to learn, develop, and strengthen certain skills and competencies to give them more confidence in possibly being a group leader. Many times, people discover existing strengths about themselves that they were unaware of by the end of the Group Leader Training.

Listed on the following pages are group leader expectations to be conscious of striving for. Again, a person does not have to be these things as much as they should be striving for them. Set your goal for trajectory. Consider the following expectations for ***Character*** and ***Ministry Focus.*** These are not absolutes written in stone. They are expectations set for our group leaders over the years that help them flourish in their ministry.

Group Leader Expectations

As a group leader, it is important to realize the responsibility and privilege that God has granted in serving Him. All Leaders must agree with and adhere to the following standards:

CHARACTER QUALITIES

To be above reproach (Titus 1:7), I will strive for/to:

- Believes in the Gospel: death, burial, & resurrection of Jesus Christ (1 Cor. 15:1-4).
- Respect from Members of the Group (Titus 2:7).
- Love & enjoyment of God & others (Matthew 22:37-39).
- Consistent maturity & growth (1 Tim. 3:1-7).
- Sober or clear-Mindedness (1 Timothy 3:2).
- Self-Control over my emotions (1 Timothy 3:2).
- Hospitality/Welcoming to strangers (1 Timothy 3:2).
- Submit to the leadership over my life. Be a member of my church (Heb. 13:7).
- Humility – open to ongoing coaching & training (Phil. 2:3-4).
- Be wise about social media posts as it is public & permanent (Phil. 1:9).
- Faithful in the little things & big things (Luke 16:10).
- Keep my word – follow through with what I say I will do (James 5:12).

- Lovingly & maturely confront others (Matthew 18:15).
- Unity – Support decisions made by my church leadership by edifying & uplifting the ministry for unity's sake (Phil. 2:2; Heb. 13:17).
- No unhealthy ideologies – value doctrine over convictions (1 Tim. 6:20).
- Generosity – give financially & faithfully to my local church (Eph. 3:10, 1 Cor. 16:2).

MINISTRY FOCUS

I will strive to:

- Share my church's vision and mission with the group.
- Shepherd & Care for my group by prioritizing:
    1. Relationships by practicing the "One Anothers".
    2. Discipling via leading discussion/teaching (Matt. 28:20).
    3. Praying (1 Thess. 5:17).
    4. Multiplying by discovering the next leader (2 Tim. 2:2).
    5. Stewarding Stories of life change (Mk. 5:19).

    Attend Quarterly Trainings.

    Be flexible – we will always do our best to respect your time.

    Show Up – Attend & learn from my group a minimum of 66% or 2/3 of the time – Consistency is Key.

    Have Fun (Prov. 15:23).

I have read the above expectations, and prayed about serving as a group leader. I agree to live them out, and feel that it is God's will for me to be a working part of the larger body in this way.

HEALTHY GROUPS PRACTICE	HEALTHY GROUPS REQUIRE
Fellowshipping – Relational	Healthy ***Leaders*** with
Growing – Transformational	• Healthy ***Doctrine***
Serving – Contribution	• Healthy ***Expectations***
Multiplying – Missional	• A ***Transformative Gospel***
	• A ***Local Church's*** Support and Oversight

Biblical Foundations Of "Healthy Groups"

GROUPS IN THE NEW TESTAMENT SCRIPTURES

The first example of a group in the New Testament Church is found in Acts 2:42-47:

> "And they devoted themselves to the apostles' teaching and the fellowship, to the breaking of bread and the prayers. And awe came upon every soul, and many wonders and signs were being done through the apostles. And all who believed were together and had all things in common. And they were selling their possessions and belongings and distributing the proceeds to all, as any had need. And day by day, attending the temple together and breaking bread in their homes, they received their food with glad and generous hearts, praising God and having favor with all the people. And the Lord added to their number day by day those who were being saved."

God designed humanity for communion with others. He created us in his very image. The blueprint of God is woven into the very core of our being. Our souls long and desire for meaningful relationships.

Have you ever considered what God was doing before he created the world? Was he lonely or bored? Did he run out of things to do with himself? At some point, did he feel the need to create something else to complete himself? No, he didn't. In fact, it is quite the opposite and speaks immensely of God's love for you and me. God had no need of creation or humanity to complete himself. He is fully sufficient, satisfied, and complete in his eternal, perfect, and holy state. At no point has God ever been lonely or ***alone*** . . . .

Since before the beginning of time, God has been in perfect, harmonious relationship with himself for all of eternity. God the Father, God the Son, and God the Holy Spirit experience awe-inspiring communion amongst one another. God's love moved him to share this with others by creating Adam and Eve and placing them in the garden of Eden, in his presence.

However, they ate of the fruit of the forbidden tree, sin entered the world, and they were cast out of the garden, but, far worse, from the ***presence of God.***

Acts 2 shifts paradigms in how God relates to his people. For the first time in history, the wedge of separation driven between God and humanity in Genesis 3 by humanity's sin is removed. The chasm of separation between humanity and God breaches. God the Son sends God the Spirit and powerfully comes upon the disciples of the early church. God's people no longer need go to the temple to be in God's presence; rather, He indwelt them. He was ***with*** them by being ***in*** them.

As seen in Acts 2:42-47, incredible works occur through the Spirit empowered and led New Testament early church. Immediately following, the first sermon of the church by Simon Peter leads three thousand to repent and be baptized. Acts 2:42-47 describes the application of their faith taking root in home groups of sorts. Groups that gathered at the temple (corporate worship) and homes (biblical community) daily were the primary practice of gospel living.

We see New Testament groups rehearse several important practices on a regular basis:

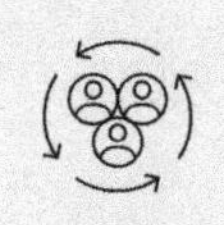

FELLOWSHIP
"devoted themselves to the breaking of bread in homes, prayers, . . . awe came upon every soul, and . . . attending the temple together."

GROW
"Devote themselves to the Apostles' teachings."

SERVE
"they were selling their belongings . . . and distributing to any as they had need."

MULTIPLY
"the Lord added to their number day by day those who were being saved."

Additional practices/attitudes:

WORSHIPFUL
"awe came upon every soul".

GRATEFUL
"with glad and generous hearts".

CONSIDERATE
"had favor with all the people".

The Group Gathering

WHAT HAPPENS IN GROUP

As you gather with your group, it's important to know why a group does what they do. What is the point of a group gathering with one another on a regular basis? How should the group interact with each other? During the group gathering, what should and shouldn't be done? What's the purpose of everything a group does? Have you answered these questions? *Thought about them?*

It's easy to start Group without considering why Groups do what they do.

Should your group do what others have done? Should it be different? Longer, shorter, deeper, more fun, or engaging? Should there be more study or fellowship? Where does prayer fit in? Should it be given more precedence or less?

Whether you're starting or strengthening a group, these are questions you've asked. If you haven't, then you are now probably asking them and a bit nervous or curious. Both can be good. Asking and answering these questions positions your group for a healthy trajectory.

Here are the primary components of a group gathering:

FELLOWSHIP	**STUDY**	**PRAYER**

Through the years of leading the Group Leader Training at churches and conferences, I have asked this question:

> "If you have 90 minutes for your group gathering, how would you divide that time up between fellowship, study, and prayer?"

By asking this question, I have elicited many different responses. Some causally stated what they had experienced in groups. Often, people's responses conflicted with one another. One participant would give most of the time to fellowship and relationship building. Another would prioritize the study. Some would minimize the prayer time as an opportunity for the gathering to be abused and hijacked by a string of unfocused trivial prayer requests. Here are some examples of how they decided to divvy up their total gathering time of 90 minutes:

	Fellowship	**Study**	**Prayer**
Option #1	60	15	15
Option #2	30	30	30
Option #3	15	60	15

Clearly, these are not the only options. There are plenty of other ways to schedule the group gathering time. The chart gives a few general examples.

STUDY

Some say the study is the most important because discipleship is all about the Word. They say...

> "Get into the Bible. We need to get into the Word of God. That's what matters most so we should spend most of our time in the study. We shouldn't waste time chit-chatting and get straight into God's Word."

FELLOWSHIP

Others say that fellowship is the most important because we must ***know*** one another. These say...

> "Building relationships is what our group's all about. We're going to be open, transparent, and confess sin to one another in our group. We aren't going to let anyone hide so we can all be known by one another."

PRAYER

Another will say that hearing about others' concerns and celebrations is vital to worshipping God. And they say...

> "How can we pray for you? We want to spend much of our time speaking to the Lord on your behalf. Our time is best spent prioritizing how we can petition on your behalf for God to work."

All three of these are good, right, and necessary to allot time to in the group gathering. However, conflict arises between these three Biblical practices when their purpose and order are misunderstood and then, therefore, misapplied.

Hence, we must ask: "What is the ***right*** amount of time to give to each Biblical practice of ***Fellowship, Study, and Prayer?"***

The answer is . . . "Yes." Allotting the ***right*** amount of time to ***study, fellowship, and prayer*** depends entirely on the season and spiritual strengths or weaknesses of your group. Here's what I mean: your group will most likely have some type of natural inclination to one of these three Biblical practices.

It will be a bit more natural for the group to engage in one of these. At the same time, there may be one or even two that are unnatural to the group. Truly, the group could even have an aversion to one or two of these Biblical practices. Most people find it easier to major in one matter as opposed to balancing for strength in all three of these practices. Therefore, as the group leader, it is essential that you understand that ***all three of these Biblical practices are equal in importance.*** However, they each have their own place to be practiced and implemented that can make them most effective during the group gathering. Whatever season your group life is in will determine how much time and emphasis you individually give to either ***fellowship, study***, or ***prayer***.

For example, you may allot more time to fellowship early on in the group as you all get to know one another to build trust. On the contrary, relationships may develop quickly and struggle to stay focused on the study. As a result, a distracted group might not gain much from the study. In response, for that season, you might focus more energy on engaging everyone in the study by allotting more time to it in preparation and facilitation. With prayer, you may find that you never actually pray as a group in any meaningful way because you run out of time. As you fellowship and discuss the study, you may sink so deep into both that prayer is forgotten. You end without prayer to respect everyone's time. For that season, you may decide to do prayer first. Even more so, you might spend an entire group praying. The group members absorb this practice into their personal spiritual life.

Conflict arises when the purpose and order of ***fellowship, study, and prayer*** are misunderstood and then, therefore, misapplied.

The group will be more predisposed to ***fellowship, study, or prayer.***

What you practice in the group gathering Models what group members will likely practice in their personal walk day to day.

As the group leader, the practices give prominence to will in turn be what the group members adopt into their own personal spiritual lives daily. You are not simply teaching or leading them for a once a week gathering. Rather, you are ***modeling*** what spiritual practices they most likely will embrace and implement in their own lives outside of the group gathering.

Model in the group gathering what you hope to see formed into the group members' everyday lives.

Truly, the greatest lesson of spiritual formation that you could possibly teach your group isn't found in the curriculum, study, or some profound truth you articulate well. Rather, it may be in the silence of what you model from one group gathering to the next.

WHY IT HAPPENS IN GROUP

We've discussed what groups should practice. Now, we'll discuss ***why*** these biblical practices are important for a group. What is their purpose? Why do they matter to the spiritual life of a group? Let me lead with this: The study isn't the only time discipleship happens in and through a group. Discipleship happens in all three of these practices: ***study, fellowship, and prayer***.

The study isn't the only time discipleship happens in a group.

FELLOWSHIP

The ***WHY*** behind fellowship is found in the Triune God and the Gospel of Jesus Christ.

The Triune God

Before all creation and humanity existed, God was never alone. For all eternity he was in perfect harmonious fellowship with God the Father, God the Son, and God the Holy Spirit. In the same way, God created humanity in his image, which left a blueprint upon us with a craving for relationship and communion (intimacy, closeness, or experienced relationship). Therefore, the Triune nature of God has modeled the perfect fellowship of not only what we innately desire, but, also, of what our fellowship with one another can, should, and gets to look like.

The Gospel

The gospel of Jesus Christ is that God sent his one and only son to humble himself by taking on human form. He submitted himself to the Father's will in perfect obedience and self-restriction of his supernatural power. Despite humanity's disobedience and depravity, God the Son came and dwelled amongst them. He did the unthinkable and sacrificed his life for the sake of humanity to be drawn near to God. Finally, through Jesus Christ's death on the cross, burial, and resurrection, he removed the separation sin had brought humanity at the fall so they could, like never before, experience the presence of God forevermore. This made possible the Holy Spirit's indwelling the believer at the moment of salvation to experience the presence of God within us. "It is no longer I who live, but Christ who lives in me."[1] The immanence (nearness) of God moving closer into intimate relationship with his chosen people is a theme seen throughout the entirety of scripture from Genesis to Revelation. ***As God moves closer to commune with us in fellowship, we as an overflow move closer to one another.*** We get to fulfill the innate relational craving of intimacy, nearness, and closeness with God's people, Christ's bride. In conclusion, we draw near in fellowship with one another because God has drawn near to us in the most unthinkable unconditionally loving way one could imagine.

The Benefits

Fellowship benefits the group and you as a group leader in several ways. First, fellowship is not just a time for people to socialize, cut up, and hang out. It's not just some culturally acceptable social norm that a group must abide by void of any spiritual purpose, or they are doing wrong. Rather, fellowship is a form of discipleship. Socializing, interacting, talking, and even joking around are all means of discipleship. In John 3:22, it says that Jesus "went into the Judean wilderness where he spent time with his disciples." Jesus spent time fellowshipping with them because he rubbed off on them. Spending time together with his disciples was a powerful form of discipleship. As a group spends time together, they will rub off on one another. Here are some spiritual benefits that fellowshipping will provide for you and your group:

FELLOWSHIP	
For the Group	**For the Group Leader**
1. Opportunity to practice what they are learning towards and with one another.	1. Gives you a pulse on where group members' hearts are prior to the study.
2. Gives space for group members to build trust with one another to share more openly.	2. Helps you know what (topics) to say, how to say it (tone), and when to say it (timing) for the study that is gathering.
3. Allows others to minister and use their gifts for the benefit of other group members.	3. Lets you build a relationship to know your group members better.
4. Demonstrations of Christlikeness are exemplified to passively challenge one another.	4. A chance to earn their trust as their group leader, as they get to see you live and lead.
As a group spends time together, they will inherently rub off on one another.	5. Earning trust softens their hearts to receive and believe what you have to say.
	6. Frees you from doing all the ministry to group members as they minister to one another relationally.

1 Galatians 2:20

Fellowship gives you, the group leader, a pulse on where someone's heart already is from their day full of experiences before arriving for the weekly group gathering. The Holy Spirit has already been working on them throughout their day. We're offered the opportunity to humbly gauge the Holy Spirit's prior work in the person and partner with Him. We can build from that existing foundation from the day of the group gathering. It's a chance to be led by the Spirit and continue His work in that person for the day, week, month, year, or longer!

Fellowship indicates what the person needs from the study time for that gathering. It helps you to know if they need to be rebuked or encouraged. Did they have a hard day or need to lament? Are they on a mountaintop craving celebration? Are they wearing shame in need of love and affirmation? Do they enter detached or indifferent with a need to be engaged and challenged? Are they on edge with stress, frustration, or anger in need of gentleness, patience, and kindness modeled towards them to center them on the peace that surpasses understanding?

Far too often, we become frustrated with people not taking our advice. Why would our correction be received when we haven't worked hard to earn the right to speak life-transforming truths into their lives? If we have not first demonstrated through our fellowship with one another that we are trustworthy, we have not yet earned the right to speak beautiful and difficult truths to be received into their lives. The famous quote, "No one cares how much you know, until they know how much you care," still rings true today. Earn their trust. Know your people as God knows and moves closer to each of us.

"Trust is gained in drops and lost in buckets."

– **JONATHAN POKLUDA**

STUDY

Additional insight will be given to this topic in training #3 – Grow. However, here are some benefits for the group:

01 Gives guidance and direction.

02 Reproves, Rebukes, and Convicts.

03 Encourages, Builds Up, and Gives Life.

04 Reveals what God says to his chosen people.

05 Includes us in God's grand story of life.

PRAYER

More discussion will follow in training #2 – Connect. Nonetheless, here's how prayer benefits you as the group leader:

1. Another opportunity to get a ***pulse*** on where a person's heart is prior to the study.
2. Lets you know how the Holy Spirit is working in a group member.
3. Shows you what group members care about.
4. It helps reveal your group member's level of maturity based on what they request prayer for.
5. At the end of the study, it allows time for them to ***worshipfully express*** what God is teaching them through the study.

QUALITIES OF A HEALTHY GROUP

In the Group Leader Training, I always ask the following question for several reasons.

Not only do we ask this in the training, but we also have our group leaders ask this question in their "First Group Gathering" as part of a group launch curriculum. Communally, it organically clarifies the purpose of the group while removing unhealthy expectations. It is intended to not only set the expectations for the group, but, in addition, it is meant to aid in training the new group to become healthy group members.

"What is one quality that makes a healthy group?"

Asking this question hundreds of times, I have been able to record the most common responses. More importantly, I have noticed a pattern of responses that are missing. I have found ***four qualities*** that have never or only been said once in over 1,500 responses:

COMMON RESPONSES

Transparency, Openness, Vulnerability, Trust, Confidentiality, Care, Acceptance, Love, Service, Humility, Teachability, Fun, Biblical.

Now, just because a response is common does not make it unimportant. These common responses are extremely important and necessary qualities for a healthy group. Here's the point of asking the question. Common responses reveal what is at the forefront of a person's thinking. Whatever is at the forefront of a person's thinking is what they consider most important. What people consider as important is what they are usually most passionate to model, teach, and strive for in a group.

COMMON RESPONSES REVEAL THE FOREFRONT OF A PERSON'S THINKING . . . .

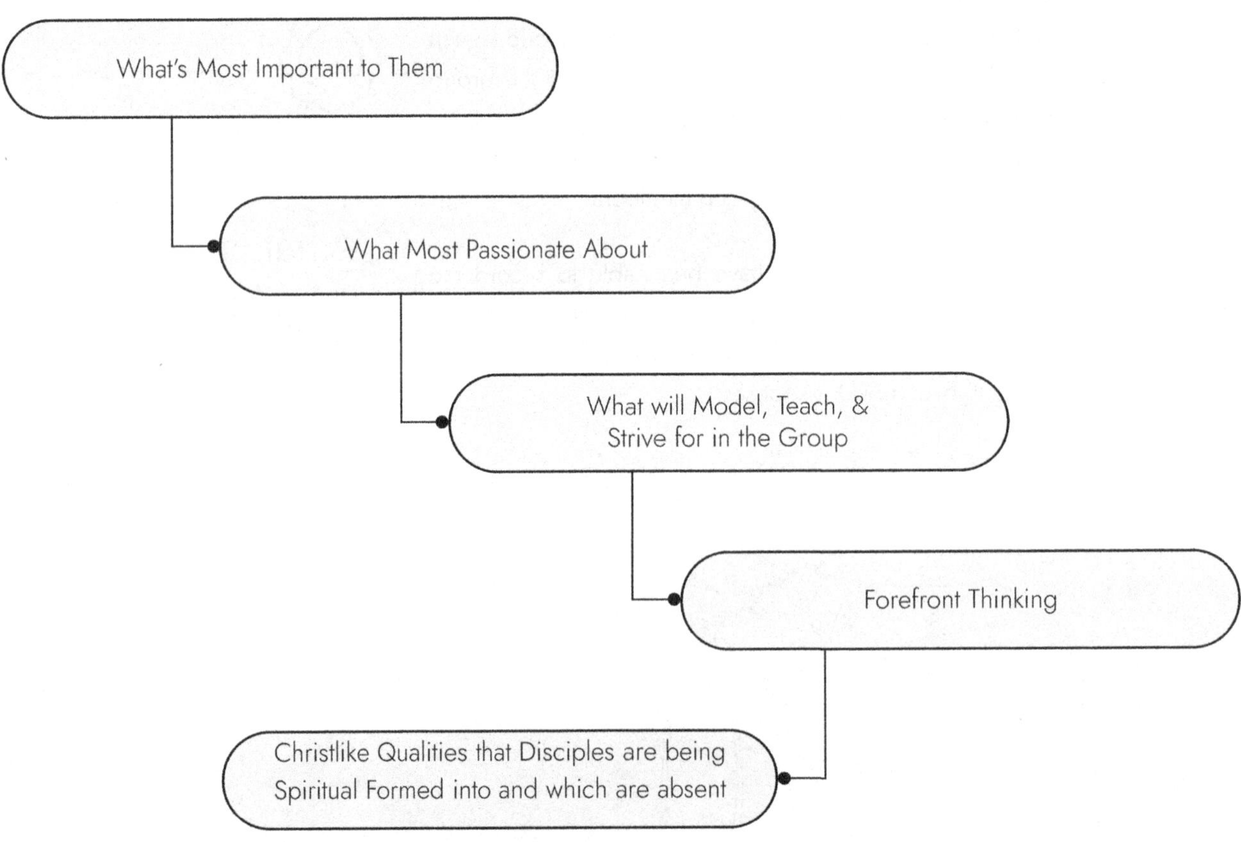

UNCOMMON RESPONSES

1. *Repentance* – Turning from one's sins post confession.
2. *Grace* – Favor towards another who's done nothing to earn it.
3. *Admonish* – Correct another with gentleness in their sin.
4. *Transformation* – Group life not centered around a Gospel of Transparency, but a Gospel of Transformation.

A Gospel of Transparency group is defined as:

"Air my dirty laundry. I'm a depraved wretch and awful human being, and it feels really good to vomit up all my sin on everyone every week at group without any life change."

There is never any progress in the person's faith, nor obedience to the teachings of Christ while being marked with constant confession without repentance to turn from their sins. It is all talk and no walk. No transformation.

A *Gospel of Transformation* group is defined as:

"Confessing my sins, repenting to turn from those sins that break my heart to talk and walk my faith. I am not a depraved wretch but am made in the image of God. By the resurrection of Christ and the life of the Spirit indwelling me, I am a new creation who is loved, holy, and righteous before God the Father. 'Day by Day, I am progressively becoming more like Christ 'from one degree of glory by another."[2]

2 2 Corinthians 3:18

GOSPEL = TRANSFORMATION

Truthfully, Christ on our behalf suffered, died on the cross, had his blood shed, paid the debt we couldn't, ransomed, redeemed, rescued, took on the wrath of God to accept the punishment rightfully due to us, and ultimately yielded up his life as a sacrifice . . . .

So that . . . .

We who believe in Christ would be viewed by God the Father as holy, righteous, redeemed, pure, beautiful, unstained, lovely, as a spotless child of His.

Jesus' Death → (leads to) → Justified

Not only did Christ die to cover our sins and pay the consequence due to us; rather, he also rose from the dead three days later to conquer sin, death, and Satan. The cross pardons the believer of their sins; the Resurrection empowers by the Spirit indwelling the believer to conquer sin, death, and Satan in their everyday lives. Christ doesn't die to leave us in the misery of our perpetual sins to reap the consequences of their offense until he returns. Rather, Christ rises from the dead to empower us with the Spirit. Now we can conquer sin, death, and Satan, to become like him in his character and nature. As we draw nearer to God, we are becoming fully genuinely human.

Jesus Risen → (leads to) → Sanctification

As group leaders, we want to be a group of Gospel Transformation that sees life change and not a Gospel of Transparency that constantly treads the waters of confession without change.

"It's ok to not be ok, but it's not ok to stay there."

– **MATT CHANDLER**

Strive to be a group of Gospel Transformation and not Transparency. Live a life reflective of Christ's resurrection and not only his death and burial.

You can change, now. Your group can be transformed by the power of Christ's resurrection today.

Essential Beliefs

There are many important beliefs, doctrines, or theological truths to be knowledgeable of as a Christ follower. Depending upon the requirements of your local church, it is not necessary to be well versed in every theological or doctrinal matter in order to lead a healthy group. Undoubtedly, there are false beliefs running amuck all through the world and even in local churches and groups. Nonetheless, it is totally possible to have a healthy group without being completely doctrinally pure and knowledgeable, so to speak.

That may sound alarming, but the truth is, no group is completely doctrinally pure and knowledgeable. We are all a work in progress.

When it comes to beliefs, doctrines, and theological matters in group life, it is most important that the essential beliefs are known and agreed upon. Amongst the group, there may be undefined ideas regarding essential beliefs. As long as there is mutual respect and submission to one another on the primary core doctrines of the faith, there can be healthy groups.

Reality is that the thought of leading a group is far more frightening than actually leading a group.

Belief does not need to be overcomplicated nor oversimplified. It does not need to be intimidating or frightening. Borrowing worry from tomorrow about possible questions of incorrect doctrine that ***could*** be said in a group discussion is an unhelpful matter to consider at this moment. Honestly, such worries are not aids to equipping and building you up to do the work of ministry – making disciples.

There are several non-negotiable essential beliefs to be knowledgeable of in order to simplify this to a proper approach to leading a group. Honestly, if you can keep the main thing at the center, much disagreement and dispute will be removed altogether. Often times, the groups that have left essential beliefs undefined are the ones that meander off into the weeds of non-essential beliefs to die on hills the New Testament never asked the Church to die on. Be knowledgeable of the essential beliefs, keep focused on and guard them firmly, but with gentleness, and ***many group issues will be resolved before they ever originate.*** Let the group become passionate for these absolute beliefs. In addition, essential beliefs make a leader spiritually healthy. God blesses and works through healthy spiritual leaders.

Healthy Essential Doctrine is the #1 Prerequisite to being a healthy group.

With all this in mind, please see the essential beliefs that follow. If you read nothing else in this chapter, please take the time to read this. It is truly vital.

TRINITY

We believe in one God eternally existing as one essence and three distinct persons: God the Father, God the Son, and God the Holy Spirit, each of whom is fully God, yet there is one God.
(Jn, 3:16-17, 14:16-17, 26; Matt. 28:19; Gen. 1; Mk. 1:9-11; Phil. 2:6-11; Acts 1:8-11, 2:1-4, 16:6-7; Rom. 5:5)

DOCTRINE OF REVELATION

God has made himself known to the world in Jesus Christ, the Scriptures (Special Revelation), and creation (General Revelation). We believe that the Bible, composed of the sixty-six books of the Old and New Testaments, is God's inspired and infallible Word. It is inerrant in the original manuscripts, and is the authority for conduct, belief, and practice.
(Heb. 1:1-2, 1 Tim. 3:16; Ps. 8; Rom. 1:20; 2 Peter 1:21)

JESUS CHRIST

We believe in the deity of Jesus Christ. We believe he is the manifestation of God in the flesh. We believe he was conceived by the Holy Spirit and born of the Virgin Mary. We believe in his sinless life and in his miracles. He is true God and true man. His death on the cross was substitutionary for mankind and paid for the sins of the world. He bodily rose from the grave, he ascended into heaven, and he will return to the earth in power and glory.
(John 1:1, 14, 18; 5:18; Heb. 1:1-9, 5:8; 1 John 5:20; 1 Tim. 2:5; 1 Cor. 15:1-5)

CREATION

We believe that God created the world from nothing and governs all things, at all times, in all places.
(Gen. 1:1-2; Ps. 24:1; Col. 1:17)

HUMANITY

We believe that all humanity is created in the image of God and possesses intrinsic dignity and worth.
(Gen. 1:27-30; 1 Cor. 10:31)

SIN

We believe that sin has fractured all things, leaving the world in desperate need of salvation.
(Gen. 3; Rom. 2:9-20; Eph. 2:1-3)

SALVATION

We believe salvation is by grace alone through faith alone in Christ alone.
(Acts 4:12; 16:31; 1 Cor. 15:1-4; Rom. 4:4-5, 5:1; 8:28-29; John 3:5-8, 16; Eph. 2:8-9; Heb. 10:19-25)

THE CHURCH

We believe that the Church is the body of Christ sent into the world to shine forth the glory of God by proclaiming the gospel and making disciples.
(1 Peter 2:9-12; Matt. 28: 18-20; Eph. 1:22, 23; 4:1-16; 1 Cor. 12:12-31)

FINAL JUDGEMENTS

We believe there is an eternal state of punishment for the unsaved and an eternal state of blessing for the saved. All unbelievers of all ages will be judged and condemned to eternal separation from God in the Lake of Fire. All believers will be saved from the wrath of God, but they will give an account of their works as God's children.
(Rom. 2:8, 9; 5:12; 2 Cor. 5:10; Heb. 9:27; Rev. 20:11-15)

THE GOSPEL

Jesus was born of the virgin Mary, lived a perfect sinless life, was tortured and crucified to take on the sins of the world. He was buried and rose three days later to conquer sin, death, and Satan, so that humanity could as well, by the indwelling relational presence of God, to bear fruit in prosperity or poverty, comfort or suffering all to the glory of God
(1 Cor. 15; Rom. 5:3-5; 1 Peter 4:12-15; Gal. 2:20)

Non-Essential Beliefs

Not only should you be aware of essential beliefs, but you may want to also be knowledgeable of non-essential beliefs. Again, it is not necessary to have a master's in theology to lead a group. Rather, there may be certain non-essential beliefs that your local church leaves open handed to allow for disagreement among believers that does not break fellowship with one another. Every local church has their own conviction on these matters. What's important to note is that it is best for you as a group leader to submit to the non-essential belief standards that your local church holds to. There may not be anything earth shattering in their non-essential list of beliefs. Nonetheless, it can be helpful to be aware of some of the beliefs they hold as non-essential so as to honor and not trample them. Again, it's helpful to be aware, not memorize. Although memorizing them can be good as well, it is not necessary to lead a healthy group.

Build Leaders. Build Groups. Build Disciples.

GROUP LEADER TRAINING #1

FINAL THOUGHTS

01. One of the best things you can do as a group leader is to be and become a healthy leader with healthy doctrine.

02. Groups of Gospel Transparency are not enough, we must strive to be and become groups of Gospel Transformation.

03. During your first group gathering, communicate and discuss what a healthy group is with your group members – it will set healthy expectations and dispel unhealthy expectations.

04. Begin strengthening your Bible reading and studying muscles. It will aid you in leading your group more comfortably.

05. Learn and know your people. Do the hard work to earn their trust so you may speak gospel truths into their lives that they receive and believe as a result of you drawing near to them.

FEEDBACK

What did you think of this training/chapter?

Please take 60 seconds or less to help us make the Group Leader Training better!

We will actually use it to make this training even better!

www.buildgroups.net/glt1feedback

GROUP LEADER TRAINING

FELLOWSHIP

02

OBJECTIVES

Answer these questions: What type of relationships should, and shouldn't we expect in a group? What is fair and unfair to expect out of relationships in a group? As a group leader, how do we help others connect to one another?

SCRIPTURE READING

1 John 1:3, 7;

New Testament "One Anothers"

TRAINING #2 CHECKLIST

- o Video
- o Fill-in-the-Blanks
- o Essential Belief Assessment
- o Group Discussion
- o Read Chapter 2

CHECKLIST 01

VIDEO

Instructions

Prior to reading the following chapter and attending your next training . . .

Go to www.buildgroups.net/glt2

. . . login, watch the video, and fill-in-the-blanks.

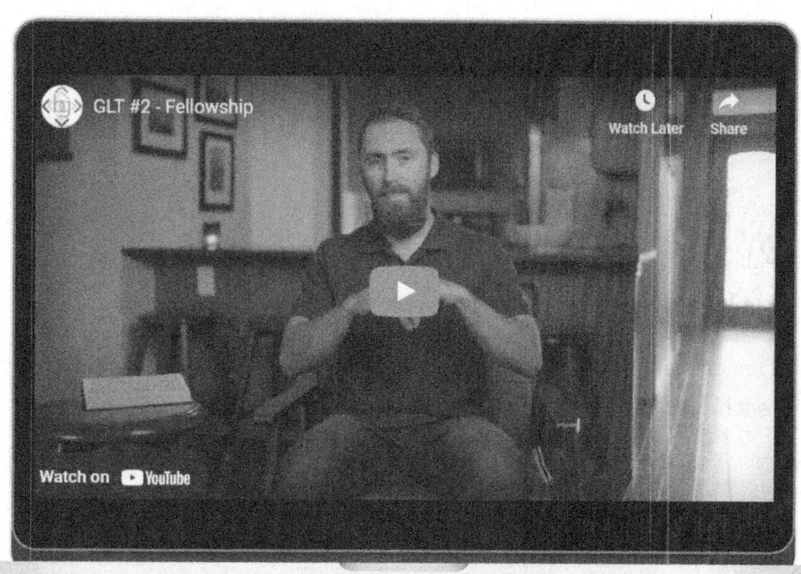

CHECKLIST 02

FILL IN THE BLANKS

Biblical Foundations of "Fellowship"

1. How is __________ different from other relationships.

    a. Matthew 22:37 – "You shall love the Lord your God with all your heart, soul, and mind."

    b. The Great Commands are to _____ God and _______ People

    c. Jesus is here on a mission.

    d. We get the privilege of having a __________ ___________ with God.

    e. That happens through _______, which is an incredible privilege we get as a Christ follower.

    f. The purpose of prayer is not just to receive and ask and request. It is to _____ with God.

    g. Don't just seek the ______ of God but the _______ of God.

2. We are supposed to pursue horizontal"Fellowship" with _________.

    a. Matthew 22:39-40 – "Love your neighbor as yourself".

    b. The Second Great Command.

    c. Fellowship with believers in Christ is _______ ________. Not temporal but forever. It's an eternal work, nothing is wasted.

    d. Demonstrated in Acts 2:42-47 – "they devoted themselves to the Apostles' teachings, fellowship, breaking of bread, & prayer."

3. What kind of ___________ should we have in group?

    a. You as the group leader set the ___________ for what the rest of the group will do.

    b. What opportunities will you provide for ________ to be built.

c. A great metric tool for measuring a healthy group that builds relationships well is answering this question, "Do people spend time together ________ of the weekly group meeting."

d. Surface-Level? Professional? Caring? Small Talk? Family Talk? Struggles? Heart-level? Business? Loving?

e. Pursue relationships that _______ through the surface.

f. Deep relationships do not happen overnight. Don't _______ relationships

g. We do not _______ community. It is _______.

h. We are created in God's image and ______ relationships with other people.

i. As God sent his one and only Son to draw near to us, we also ought to _______ _______ to one another.

CHECKLIST 03

ESSENTIAL BELIEF ASSESSMENT

Purpose

To expose and give people the opportunity to explore the essential beliefs or doctrines of the Christian faith. This is not a pass or fail exam; but, rather, it is a chance to learn important Biblical beliefs together.

		True	False	Unsure
01	The Gospel is that Jesus died and rose physically (bodily) from the dead to conquer sin, death, and Satan.	☐	☐	☐
02	God counts a person as righteous not because of one's works but only because of one's faith in Jesus Christ.	☐	☐	☐
03	Religious belief is a matter of personal opinion; it is not about objective truth.	☐	☐	☐
04	The Bible is 100% accurate in all that it teaches.	☐	☐	☐
05	Even the smallest sin deserves eternal damnation.	☐	☐	☐
06	Humanity is created in the image of God who is sufficient in and of himself and needs no one or anything else to sustain him; therefore, humanity has no need of relationships with other believers.	☐	☐	☐
07	The Holy Spirit is a force but is not a personal being.	☐	☐	☐
08	Hell is a real place where certain people will be punished forever.	☐	☐	☐
09	Jesus is the first and greatest being created by God.	☐	☐	☐
10	Despite suffering and evil in the world, God is good and blameless in his nature.	☐	☐	☐

Refer to this link for the answer guide: https://www.buildgroups.net/eba2

CHECKLIST 04

GROUP DISCUSSION

1A. Introductions (if participants haven't met)

- Name
- Family
- What you do for work?
- What group are you in?
- How long have you been at this church?

1B. Icebreaker (if participants have met) If you were a pro wrestler, what would be your entrance theme song?

2. What were your thoughts on the video?

3. Quick Hitter Question: In 60 seconds or less, what does a relationship with God look like?

4. What is the purpose of prayer?

5. We've discussed vertical relationships. Now let's discuss horizontal relationships with one another. What does it look like to connect with other people?

6. What kind of connections should we have in a group?

7. What is community? What's the difference between community and Biblical community?

8. How do we strive for deeper connections?

9. Despite good intentions to build relationships, conflict is sure to arise. Is conflict a bad thing to be avoided or is there good that can come from it?

10. How can you help group members connect to one another and not only yourself?

CHECKLIST 04

FELLOWSHIP

BIBLICAL FOUNDATIONS

WE ARE TO FELLOWSHIP WITH GOD

"You shall love the Lord your God with all your heart, soul, and mind."

– **MATTHEW 22:37**

The Great Commandment. No GREATER Commandment. We get the privilege of having a vertical relationship with God. That happens through several means. We get access to God, which is the greatest blessing of the Christ follower. It is how we have a relationship with God. Prayer is not just asking *for.* It is being with God.

WE ARE TO FELLOWSHIP WITH PEOPLE

"Love your neighbor as yourself."

– **MATTHEW 22:39-40**

The Second Great Command. We get to have horizontal relationships with people.

This is demonstrated in Acts 2:42-47. "They devoted themselves to the Apostle's teachings, fellowship, breaking of bread, and prayer." Fellowship is the eternal union of believers to God and one another through Christ by the Holy Spirit.

WHAT KIND OF RELATIONSHIPS?

Surface Level? Professional? Caring? Small Talk? Family Talk? Share Struggles? Heart Level? Business? Loving? We should Strive for deep relationships.

"For God is my witness, how I ***yearn*** for you all with the affection of Christ Jesus."

– **PHILIPPIANS 1:8**

The phrase "One Another" is said almost 60 times in the New Testament. Nearly every time the phrase "One Another" is used in the New Testament it is meant to describe what Christian community should look like among believers. <u>It is a prescribed way Christians should conduct their lives in community together.</u> Specifically, it is not a discussion if Christians will be in community with "One Another." Rather, it is assumed that Christians will "be in community with 'One Another.'" It is an understood fact of the Christian life that believers will live out life together in Biblical community.

These are significant because they informed the early church on how they were to conduct themselves in community with one another.

"ONE ANOTHERS" OF THE NEW TESTAMENT

"Love One Another" x 15					
"Encourage"	x 5	"Live in harmony"	x 1	"Be devoted"	x 1
"Greet"	x 4	"Pray"	x 1	"Be patient"	x 1
"Be humble"	x 3	"Don't slander"	x 1	"Be gentle"	x 1
"Forgive"	x 2	"Don't judge"	x 1	"Admonish"	x 1
"Have the Mind of Christ"	x 2	"Don't deprive"	x 1	"Spur to love"	x 1
"Live in peace"	x 2	"Don't lie"	x 1	"Be kind"	x 1
"Bear in love"	x 2	"Accept"	x 1	"Don't grumble"	x 1
"Have compassion"	x 2	"Confess"	x 1	"Do good"	x 1
"Agree"	x 1	"Instruct"	x 1	"Honor"	x 1
"Be like minded"	x 1	"Offer hospitality"	x 1	"Serve"	x 1
"Don't pay back wrong"	x 1	"Don't provoke"	x 1	"Speak songs"	x 1
"Have equal concern"	x 1	"Be sympathetic"	x 1	"Build up"	x 1
"Spur to good deeds"	x 1				

Biblical community is the "One Anothers" of the New Testament.

"So, God created man in his own image, in the image of God he created them, male and female he created them."

- GENESIS 1:27

The TRINITY is an ETERNITY of CONNECTING between God the Father, God the Son, and God the Holy Spirit.

Before humanity existed, God was in perfect harmonious FELLOWSHIP with God the Father, God the Son, and God the Holy Spirit.

Being created in the image of God, humanity is hardwired for relationship with others.

FELLOWSHIP TODAY

Fellowship today looks vastly different than how it was done in the New Testament time period. In modern day, there is a host of new ways and manners to fellowship with one another.

The book of Acts is ***de***scriptive, not ***pre***scriptive. The Gospel message and teachings of Christ are unchanging.

Our methods are adapting in many ways. As culture changes, our methods do as well. We adapt our methods to culture, not our message. Knowing HOW to connect people to one another is essential.

It is not optional or an additional accessory of bells and whistles to a better Christian life. Rather, it is essential if Christians are to grow into Christlikeness.

"FELLOWSHIP" WITH GOD

HOW DO WE HAVE A RELATIONSHIP WITH GOD?

A relationship with God is doing and being.

DOING	BEING
You can serve your spouse all you want by washing dishes, changing diapers, sweeping floors, working a job, folding laundry, paying bills, doing house repairs, but if you never talk to your spouse, you probably don't and won't have a good marriage.	On the other hand, you can talk to your spouse all day, dream together, make promises, but if you don't follow through by serving them, then your words are empty, and you probably don't and won't have a great marriage.

THE PURPOSE OF PRAYER	
A	Adoring God
C	Confessing Sin to God
T	Thanking God
S	Supplicating/ Asking God

A relationship with God includes doing and being with him. Duty and Delight

Prayer isn't only seeking the hand of God; it's seeking the face of God.

– - **DANIEL HENDERSON**

Most often, it is believed that prayer is the genie in a lamp we rub to wish for whatever our heart's desire. Whether it be earthly or eternal, many think that's how prayer works. Nothing could be further from the truth.

Prayer serves as our primary means to communicate and have a relationship with God. Being brought near to God by the Holy Spirit indwelling us through the death and resurrection of Jesus Christ, we now can personally go to God unstained from any sin without separation and be with him.

Prayer is the connection that we didn't have prior to Christ. It is how we personally fellowship with God. Even more powerfully, it is how we fellowship with God together.

Praying in group together can be a powerful and transformative experience. Not just the routine, "Let's start group off with a prayer." Rather, attempting something a little bit different than the routine, traditional, say the same words without any heart behind it type of prayer.

DIFFERENT WAYS TO PRAY IN GROUP	
Challenge 01	Instead of praises and prayer requests, take those 15 minutes of sharing and pray your praises and requests as a group one by one.
Challenge 02	Pray for the person sitting to your left and go around a circle for everyone to pray over another.
Challenge 03	Each gathering choose one person or couple to lay hands on and pray over specifically.

"FELLOWSHIP" WITH GOD'S PEOPLE

HOW DO WE HAVE COMMUNITY WITH OTHERS?

The "One Anothers" of the New Testament are commanded. Biblical community isn't something that is ***found***; it's ***built***. It's not about finding the ***"right"*** group. Building biblical community takes hard work, time, intentionality, risk, patience, gentleness, love, grace, and more . . . "One Anothering" is Biblical Community.

COMMUNITY VS BIBLICAL COMMUNITY

What is the difference between "Community" and "Biblical Community?" Is there a difference or are they the same? Can the CrossFit community produce and offer the same thing as a local church small group? No, they cannot. Here are the differences.

COMMUNITY	**BIBLICAL COMMUNITY**
	Fellowship
Friendship	Gospel
	N.T. "One Anothers"
Natural	Supernatural
Spiritless	Holy Spirit
Culturally Subjective	Biblically Authoritative
Exclusive to Outsiders	Inclusive to Outsiders
Temporary Relationships	Eternal Relationships

WHAT KIND OF RELATIONSHIPS SHOULD WE STRIVE FOR?

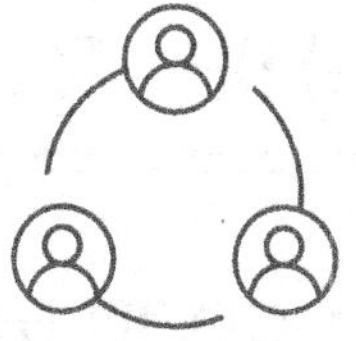

Relationships Cannot Be Microwaved

Connect with others at the level they are comfortable connecting at and at the pace they desire as well.

Connect with the ***intention of moving deeper*** in the relationship – always strive for deeper relationships.

Be Patient, as building relationships/Biblical community takes time.

Manage your own expectations well, knowing that not every group is the same. Not every group will go as deep as you've experienced in prior relationships.

Manage their expectations well, as all have different expectations as to why they join a group and what they hope to get out of it. Here are some unhealthy and unrealistic examples of what people hope to get out of a group:

> *Best Friend For Life* (B.F.F.L) – No one is ***promised*** to find their B.F.F.L. It's possible, but that is not the goal or definition of a successful group.
>
> *Deep study, no feelings* – Others will want an in-depth Bible study without ***heart work*** such as confession of sins or transparency of weakness to share their struggles.
>
> *Personal Counselor* – There is the person who hopes the group will be their personal spiritual counselors with incredible wisdom. As a result, the person is sorely disappointed when they don't find amazing godly counselors of the Lord's wisdom to be shared with them.
>
> *Find or forge community* – Many hope they can discover amazing community that they can slide themselves right into, but didn't do any of the hard work to build. Community isn't ***found***, it is only ***forged*** together with others in a group through practicing the "One Anothers" of the New Testament.

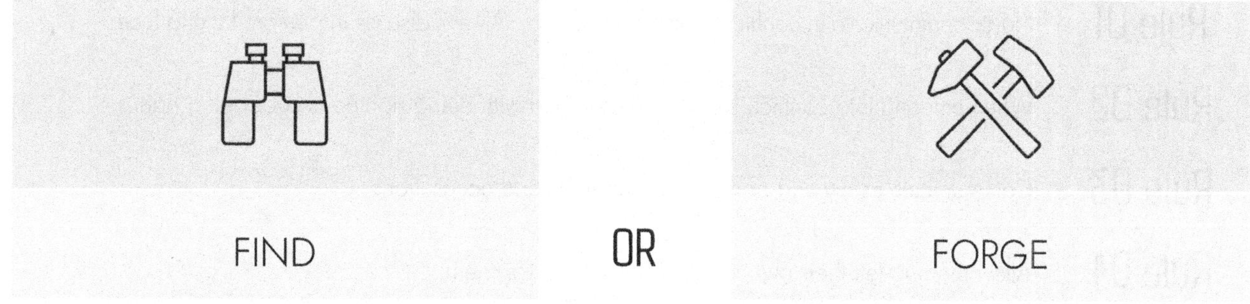

"FELLOWSHIP" THROUGH CONFLICT

CONFLICT? A GOOD THING?

When we strive for deeper relationships, conflict is certain to arise between a diverse group of people with differing backgrounds, beliefs, and baggage. Conflict isn't innately bad. Conflict is Gospel Opportunity. We can't avoid or love conflict, but we must embrace it.

Offense = Opportunity

Conflict leads to Gospel Opportunities such as forgiving, being patient, caring, admonishing, and being long-suffering towards one another.

When there is conflict amongst group members, it tends to ***bind them closer together*** as they handle it biblically and reconcile in love.

Conflict is the fast lane to Relationship Building.

Conflict most often leads to a ***greater understanding of one another's*** thought process, actions, and heart.

Conflict forces us to ***communicate better*** with one another.

It can ***grow and sanctify*** the group in exponential ways!

When conflict comes it is a gospel opportunity for gospel reconciliation.

Don't write the person's story for them, let them tell it.

HOW TO COMMUNICATE IN CONFLICT

Rule 01	Never communicate in conflict behind a keyboard. Always discuss in person, face to face.
Rule 02	When entering into conflict, be more concerned with being righteous over being right.
Rule 03	Communicate safely and not with assumptions and accusations
Rule 04	Allow them to tell their own story; don't write it for them.
Rule 05	Listen with an open heart and trust the Holy Spirit to convict and guide as needed.

"I wanted to talk to you and ask because it seems to me that . . . __________ . . . am I accurately seeing that or am I misinterpreting you in that way?

"I want to better understand your perspective. Please, help me see where you're coming from."

OUT OF MY DEPTH

WHEN I CAN'T HELP

There are times in group when a person requires help, care, and attention that you are incapable of giving.

Some misconceive that the group leader should be able to handle any issue that arises in a group. However, that's just not true.

Are you trained in how to handle marital affairs, divorces, death of a child, spouse, or friend? How about drug, porn, or alcohol addictions? Are you licensed to counsel mental health disorders such as bipolar, clinical depression, or O.C.D.?

You are out of your depth.

Chances are no one is trained in all these areas nor are most trained in just one of these areas.

If you need more convincing, here are a few reasons why you should not attempt to be the primary care source for a group member in these deep shark infested waters. It can drown the entire group.

When a group member has a burden, trial, or habitual sin out of your depth such as previously listed, it is wise to seek outside care assistance for the group member. Now, that does not mean you kick them out of the group. It does not mean that you don't pray, discuss, and love on them as a group. Rather, you allow them to go to a setting with someone who will be most helpful for restoring them from their issue.

If you try to be the primary source of care for the group member, it will turn into a complete mess. Why? Because your group members are not trained in how to care for someone going through a divorce or experiencing layered levels of grief. They are not equipped to counsel others through mental health disorders.

Group leaders are not meant to handle, help, or fix every group member issue.

When the group purpose shifts from community to a specialized care of one group member, everyone loses what they joined a group for in the first place – community. Your group members didn't sign up to serve in a care ministry. They joined to find community with other believers. Again, this does not mean that you shouldn't walk through hard things together in group. Walking through difficulty together is completely recommended and necessary to build biblical community with one another. It is the difficulty that is out of your depth that needs a hand off to someone specially trained to help them. Don't try to be the primary source of care. Rather, be a secondary source that allows you to pray, encourage, love, and build up the person. While they can get more specialized help that helps in their greatest moments of turmoil. Let your group be a group. Also, let the struggling group member be in a safe place to get them help they need.

Untrained groups are more likely to hurt than help with issues out of their depth.

WHAT CAN I DO?

So, the question becomes, what do you do? As the group leader, when a group member has an issue that is out of your depth, what do you do?

A sure way to kill a group is by changing the purpose of the group to something the group has never been trained for.

Groups are not the answer for every person's individual problem. Rather, groups fulfill a very specific purpose – community. There are other ministries that offer training and curriculum to help navigate people through difficult issues the average Christian and group leader is incapable of.

Here's a few ideas on how you can handle these specific issues:

Divorce or death of a loved one – there are great curriculums available such as Divorce Care (www.divorcecare.org) or Grief Share (www.griefshare.org) that a care leader could take a group member through. Or, if there is no one willing to lead that type of a ministry or care group at your church, there are listings online of other churches that offer it locally (www.divorcecare.org/findagroup) (www.griefshare.org/findagroup) and virtual Zoom groups that remove all geographical challenges.

Drug, porn, or alcohol addiction – there are solid curriculums available for these matters also. Celebrate Recovery is for those with hurts, habits, and hang ups (www.celebraterecovery.com). If there is no one willing to lead this at your local church, you can find offerings at other churches or virtual Zoom options online (https://locator.crgroups.info/) . In addition, it is always best to take these matters to your pastor at your local church. They often know of other areas of assistance nearby that can help. For example, a group member may need a rehabilitation facility. Your pastor may have good recommendations.

Mental health disorders – can be very specialized instances that are wisest to search for help. Two important notes. One, diagnosed mental health disorders are not sin issues that can be prayed, served, or scripturally read away. Mental health disorders are no different than a broken bone. We seek common grace medical attention if available, not preach scripture at it to stop being broken. Two, there are many over diagnosed people who are put on psychotropic drugs that numb the broken organ without ever healing it. Seeking out a Christian counselor who is slow to put someone on psychotropic drugs, but not averse to it can be a balanced approach to help. If a group member is seeking help with a mental health disorder in the group, it is best to bring your pastor into the conversation. They may have counselors or therapists they would recommend. It is also good to note that not every counselor or therapist is the correct one for a group member. Each one has their own specialty such as marriage, addictions, trauma, children, etc. Someone with O.C.D. is best paired with an O.C.D. specialist. In these matters, it is wisest to seek outside aid to best serve the group member and the group on a whole.

CONNECTING TO CARE

Now, the awkward part can be engaging a group member to consider one of these supplemental support groups. Fearfully, you might assume they're going to feel like you're offloading them to be someone else's problem and perceived as uncaring. It can be a tricky matter to navigate them to a ministry that can help. However, it is completely worth it in the long run. First, it is best to identify or have the individual confirm in saying what their given struggle is. If they are unaware or have not openly admitted to the struggle, it is more difficult to enter the conversation of aid for them, but not impossible. Self-admission allows you to speak into it more easily.

Once you identify the issue, you can seek outside help from your pastor or another ministry that better suits helping the group member's need. When you have the conversation with the group member, be ready to connect them with a person's contact info and how they can take their next step to get help.

When you have the conversation with your group member, there are a few things you want to emphasize:

LOVE
Let the group member know that you all love them and want to help them.

WELCOME
They are welcome to your group and that you don't and won't love them any differently because of their struggle.

DIRECT
The group is not equipped to best serve their primary need and that there are other ministries that can meet their need.

PARTNER
Emphasize this is not a goodbye. Rather, it is a step of greater reliance upon and bearing one another's burdens together. Stress that the group will continue to pray for, encourage, and build them up as they receive specialized assistance to overcome their struggle.

COMMUNITY
Emphasize they are not losing their community with the group. Instead, they are strengthening it and will continue to belong to the group.

(Unless there are severe or extreme circumstances, then it may be best for the individual to leave your group while they receive aid)

Once you have had the conversation with them, be sure to give them a clear next step and a person to reach out to via text or email. Send a three-way text or email introducing the group member to the person or ministry. Small efforts such as these can go a long way for struggling group members to take the next step, feel cared for, and not inconsiderately handed off as someone else's problem to deal with.

"FELLOWSHIP" TODAY

FELLOWSHIP GATHERINGS

It's important to have gatherings that solely consist of fellowshipping together. Eating a meal and having conversation with no study for people to unwind and relax is disarmingly crucial to connecting with one another.

It can't be about business or the study every time you gather. A great motto to approach your group with is: *"Be a friend first."*

GAME NIGHTS

Once more, it's important that your group doesn't just study together. In addition, it is essential that you all have fun together. Laughter, fun, and enjoyment are certainly all things Jesus had with his disciples.

Fun helps build relationships in ways a study cannot.

SOCIAL MEDIA

Friend Request group members. Share moments and life experiences on your life highlight reel (Facebook, Twitter, Instagram, etc.).

Another option to connect outside of the group gathering time is to create a private social media group chat via GroupMe, Facebook, Messenger, etc. for another opportunity for people's lives to intersect and have a reason to connect with one another.

TAKE ATTENDANCE

The role of a shepherd and pastor is to faithfully steward and tend to the flock of God. It is very difficult to shepherd people if you or your pastor do not know who belongs to your group and potentially to your local church.

It is best to shepherd your group ***together in unity***. Don't shepherd your group in ***isolation*** from the larger church body, or you will end up putting more weight of responsibility on yourself than you will be able to bear. Trust your pastoral leadership. They want to help you shepherd well.

Taking attendance helps them to know who is unconnected. Knowing this allows them to work on connecting the unconnected to a group to begin building Biblical community with others.

CONNECT GROUP MEMBERS TO ONE ANOTHER

It's one thing to connect with people yourself; it's a totally different thing to know ***how to help others*** connect with one another.

	Dependent ⟶	**Independent** ⟶	**Interpendent**
HAS	A friendship with the Group Leader	Biblical Community	Biblical community with potential new group leaders
MISSING	Biblical Community	More than one Biblical leader	Biblical Multiplication
EXAMPLE	UNSUSTAINABLE	SUSTAINABLE	REPRODUCIBLE

You cannot be the only one who has all the relationships, nor can you singlehandedly be the glue that holds the whole group together. This approach is ***unsustainable*** and is not "One Anothering" or biblical community. Introduce group members to one another. Think of ***common interests*** group members have and help them connect the dots. ***Give them a reason to talk to one another*** and help them start to build a relationship. Help them begin to build a relationship by asking good questions.

ASK GOOD QUESTIONS

Where are you from? What do you do for fun?

Where do you work? Do you have any family?

How is your family? How's your day going?

Have you been coming to ______ church awhile?

Are you a sports fan? What area do you live in?

"Many hands make light work."
- John Heywood

"FELLOWSHIP WITH YOUR GROUP

THERE ARE WAYS TO "CONNECT" YOUR GROUP THAT YOU ALREADY DO.

Here are some examples:

1. *Group text* – Shoot out a mid-week text to spark conversation outside group gathering time (depending on your group size – maybe start a few group texts between men, women, spouses).

2. *Text confirmations* – Text ahead of time to confirm people are attending the group gathering time.

3. *Recap emails* – Send out to all group members with a recap of the prior gathering's study and a sneak preview of what you will be covering in the upcoming week's study.

4. *Food & Beverages* – People are more likely to attend and feel more comfortable if some form of food and drink is provided. Don't break the bank to provide it every gathering yourself. Instead, invite everyone to bring something. There could even be an informal dinner together prior to the study.

5. *Include as you do life* – With a social media post or group text, say, "Heading to lunch after church, let us know if you'd like to join" (This is an "as you go" type of connecting).

6. *You Version Bible App* – Start a group reading plan together.

7. Collect phone numbers from all group members and be sure they each have one another's contact info.

8. Text people on their *birthday.*

9. *Friend request or follow* group members.

10. *Pray* for your group.

11. *Host a party* in your home or another group member's.

12. Catch up at Sunday services. Maybe even try to sit together in the same worship service.

13. *Post group photos* on your personal social media (show people your group is a highlight of your week!).

14. *Think about* people in your group.

15. ***Ice Breaker games*** or activities can help disarm and loosen people up to connect better during the group gathering time or a fellowship night.

16. Be kid-friendly and conscientious.

17. ***Play games*** like Cornhole, Catch Phrase, Spoons, Heads Up, Two Truths and a Lie, Pictionary, Apple to Apples. Choose games that can include all group members, allow conversation, and games that don't require much skill or focus for members to enjoy the presence of one another.

Build Leaders. Build Groups. Build Disciples.

GROUP LEADER TRAINING #2

FINAL THOUGHTS

01. One of the best things you can do as a group leader is to ***manage your own expectations*** well, knowing that not every group is the same. Not every group will go as deep as you desire or have experienced previously. You may not have the same connections or potentially have a deep connection at the pace you desire initially or long-term.

02. As the group leader, you can set a great trajectory for your group by ***setting and communicating clear expectations*** of what people can expect in your group from the beginning. As new people join, it's wise to reshare these expectations as a reminder to the entire group. An occasional email with the purpose and expectations of the group can help unify everyone into same mindedness for ***group harmony.***

03. Be okay with heart-level discussion taking three to six months to work people up into sharing more personal matters than simply small talk and everyday events in their life. Be longsuffering and patient, but don't be afraid to model heart-level discussion. Challenge them by setting the example.

FEEDBACK

What did you think of this training/chapter?

Please take 60 seconds or less to help us make the Group Leader Training better!

We will actually use it to make this training even better!

www.buildgroups.net/glt2feedback

GROUP LEADER TRAINING

GROW

03

OBJECTIVES

Answer these questions: What should we desire to grow in? How do we help others grow in their spiritual maturity? What milestones are there for growing? How can group be a place for members to grow into greater Christlikeness?

SCRIPTURE READING

Ephesians 4:11-16

TRAINING #3 CHECKLIST

- o Video
- o Fill-in-the-Blanks
- o Essential Belief Assessment
- o Group Discussion
- o Read Chapter 3

CHECKLIST 01

VIDEO

Instructions

Prior to reading the following chapter and attending your next training . . .

Go to www.buildgroups.net/glt3

. . . login, watch the video, and fill-in-the-blanks.

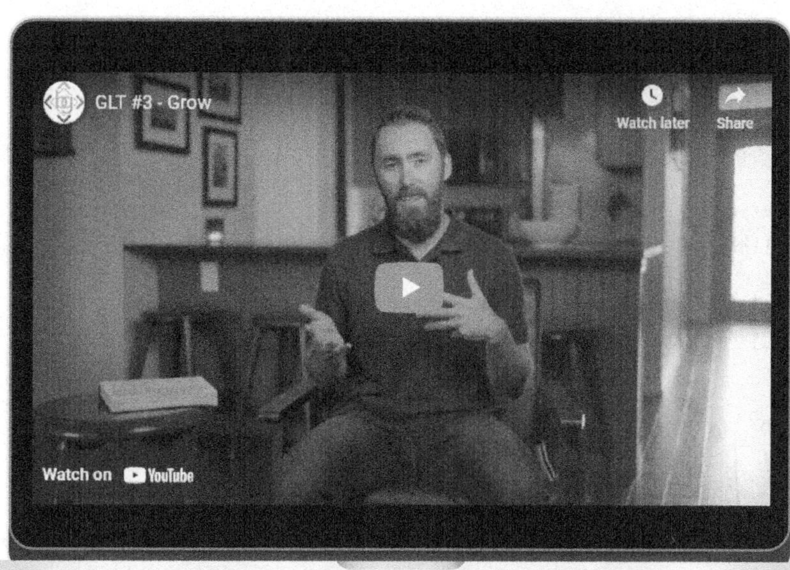

CHECKLIST 02

FILL IN THE BLANKS

Biblical Foundations of "Grow"

A. You must have ______ _________ in order to grow.

   a. We hardwired to __________.

   b. You desire to grow in something ____________.

   c. Examples: athletics, knowledge, work place, skills, board games, sports, relationships, bank accounts, video games, marriage, etc.

B. Read Ephesians 4:11-16

   a. Biblical community and biblical knowledge are __________ for spiritual growth.

   b. John 1:14 – "the only Son, from the Father, full of grace & truth"

C. As we grow, we become more _________ to biblical commands.

D. Jesus did not instantly __________ his disciples with the snap of a finger.

E. There are _______ stages in the discipleship process Jesus takes his disciples through.

F. Our goal is to help people move from the consumer and into the __________.

G. Let the __________ process of discipleship of how people mature at the pace God determines.

H. _________ every step towards spiritual maturity your group members take.

I. Raise that ___________ and say, "Thus far the Lord has brought me. Praise God! Look what he has done! Look at his faithfulness in how he is _________ you."

J. When we have Healthy Leaders, we will have the opportunity to Build Healthy Groups. Then, we can Build Healthy Disciples Together.

CHECKLIST 03

ESSENTIAL BELIEF ASSESSMENT

PURPOSE

To expose and give people the opportunity to explore the essential beliefs or doctrines of the Christian faith. This is not a pass or fail exam; but, rather, it is a chance to learn important Biblical beliefs together.

		True	False	Unsure
01	Jesus was a great teacher, but he was not God.	☐	☐	☐
02	Even though God doesn't have to, He is faithful to rescue, redeem, and restore his rebellious creation.	☐	☐	☐
03	The Holy Spirit can tell me to do something which is forbidden in the Bible.	☐	☐	☐
04	Jesus Christ's death on the cross is the only sacrifice that could remove the penalty of my sin.	☐	☐	☐
05	There will be a time when Jesus Christ returns to judge all the people who have lived.	☐	☐	☐
06	The Bible, like all sacred writings, contains helpful accounts of ancient myths but is not literally true.	☐	☐	☐
07	Gender identity is a matter of choice.	☐	☐	☐
08	Learning about theology is for pastors and scholars only.	☐	☐	☐
09	Abortion is a sin, but not unforgivable.	☐	☐	☐
10	God will always reward true faith with material blessings in this life.	☐	☐	☐

Refer to this link for the answer guide: https://www.buildgroups.net/eba3

CHECKLIST 04

GROUP DISCUSSION

1. What were your thoughts on the video?

2. Quick Hitter Question: In 60 seconds or less, what is something you desire to grow in currently?

3. What is something (person, event, book, circumstance, etc.) God has used to grow you recently?

4. We've discussed what has grown you. Now, let's discuss how we can help others grow. How can you help others grow?

5. We cannot reach where we're going until we know where we are. How can we identify where someone is in their spiritual maturity?

6. What are some indicators to help us identify? What are some things you could listen or watch for?

7. Once we identify where someone is in their spiritual maturity, how do we know what their next step is?

8. What are some potential dangers that could arise in our hearts as we identify others' sins and offenses?

CHECKLIST 04

GROW

BIBLICAL FOUNDATIONS

HUMAN HARDWIRE

We all ***desire*** to grow in something.

> Examples: knowledge, athletics, career, skills, board games, relationships, bank accounts, video games, marriage, parenting, etc.

What are we to grow in as Christ followers?

How are we to grow?

In John 1:38, Jesus asks two disciples who approach him, "What are you seeking?" A more literal translation would be, "What do you want?"

Before we take steps to grow, we must ask ourselves this question. "What do I want?" By default, what we want, desire, or long for is what we will work for and move towards. Jesus is no stranger to this. Human desires and emotions are far more compelling to complex human beings than logic or intellect. At the core of the Christian faith, our desire, our want, is for God.

"What we desire is what we naturally gravitate towards."[3]

– JOHN K.A. SMITH

3 "You Are What You Love," James K.A. Smith

WE ARE TO GROW IN TWO THINGS: *LOVING GOD & PEOPLE.*

"You shall love the Lord your God with all your heart, soul, and mind. This is the first and great commandment. And a second is like it: you shall love your neighbor as yourself. On these two commandments depend on the law and the prophets."

- MATTHEW 22:37-40

Fellowship ***vertically*** with God and ***horizontally*** with people. We should not just ***have*** vertical and horizontal relationships. In addition, we should be growing our vertical and horizontal relationships.

We are called to grow in ***grace*** and ***knowledge*** of God.

"But grow in the grace and knowledge of our Lord and Savior Jesus Christ."

- 2 PETER 3:18

We are called to grow in ***spiritual maturity*** of Christ.

"We are to grow up in every way into Him."

- EPHESIANS 4:15

"Him we proclaim, warning everyone and teaching everyone with all wisdom, that we may present everyone mature in Christ."

– **COLOSSIANS 1:28**

"...the only Son, from the Father, full of ***grace*** and ***truth***."

– **JOHN 1:14**

HOW DO WE GROW?

We are called to grow ***together***.

"And they devoted themselves to the apostles' teachings and the fellowship, to the breaking of bread . . . and all who believed were together."

– **ACTS 2:42-47**

Self-examination helps us grow in Christlikeness.

"Therefore, we must pay much closer attention to what we have heard, lest we drift away from it."

– HEBREWS 2:1

"Examine yourselves, to see whether you are in the faith. Test yourselves."

– 2 CORINTHIANS 13:5

How do we help others identify where they are in their spiritual maturity of Christlikeness?

One way to help you self-examine and identify others is with a tool called "The Table of Spiritual Maturity." The ***Table*** is a grid to help ***identify*** where you are in your spiritual growth of Christlikeness.

"The Table" can help set and determine if we are on the right trajectory of growing into more Christlikeness or not. It's like using the mall map without knowing where the "You Are Here" star is. "The Table" can be our "You Are Here" location finder to grow more in Christlikeness.

There are several seats at the table and our goal is to get ourselves and others all the way around the table.

We must ask, "Where am I at the Table?"

You need to know where ***you*** are before you can go around the Table.

In most cases, you need to go around the Table before you can ***take others*** around the Table yourself.

Jesus took his disciples through four stages of growth. He helped his disciples ***identify*** where they were at the Table.

THE TABLE OF SPIRITUAL MATURITY

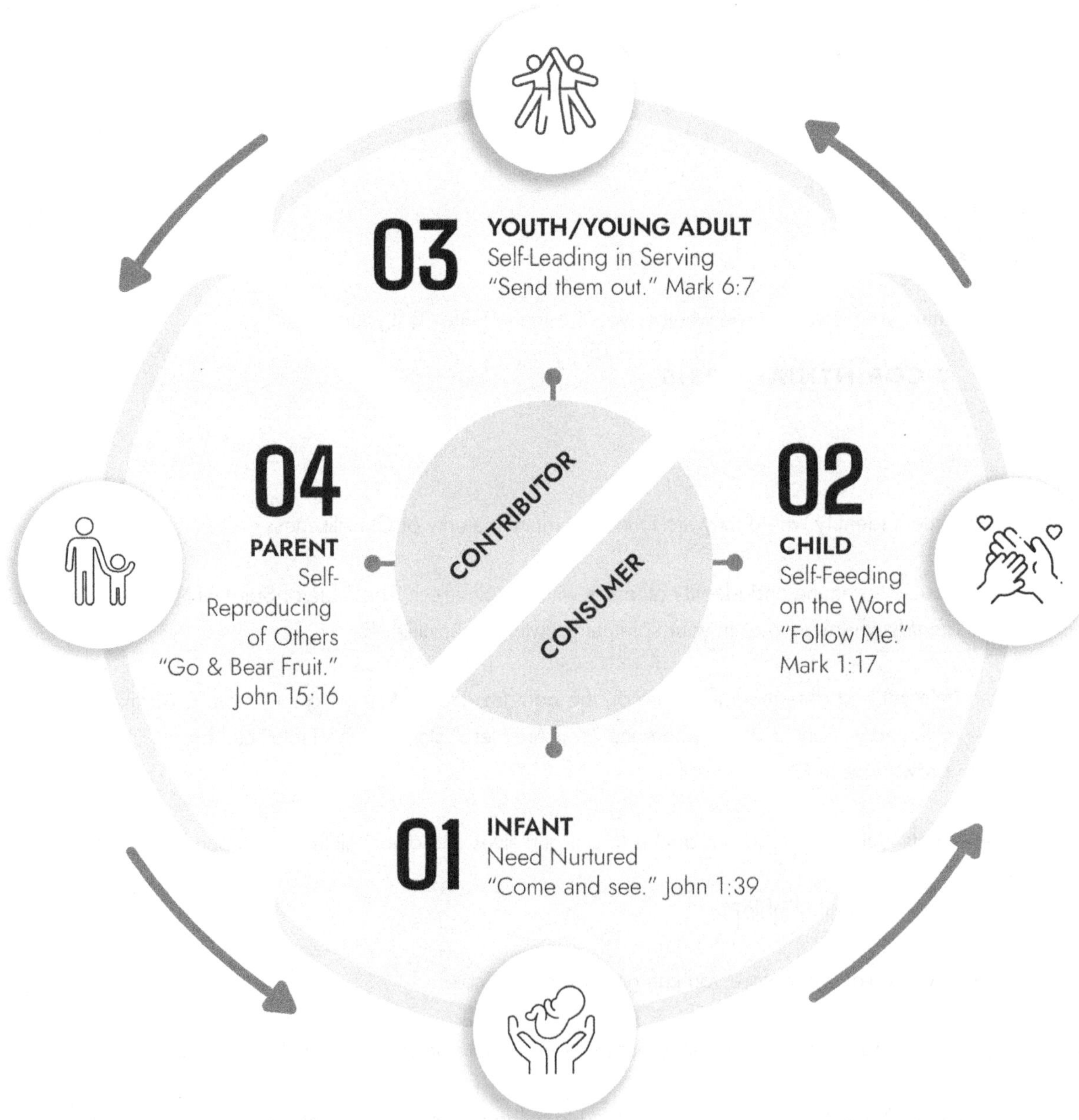

4 SEATS AT THE TABLE

Here is the Biblical Model and Example:

INFANT
"Come & See" – John 1:39

CHILD
"Follow Me" – Mark 1:17

YOUTH/YOUNG
"Send Them Out" – Mark 6:7

ADULT/PARENT
"Go & Bear Fruit" – John 15:16

You must know where you are before you can become what you want.

HELPING OTHERS GROW

RECOGNIZING PROGRESS

Often, helping others grow into greater Christlikeness can feel like catching wind. One moment it's there, the next it is gone. It seems so elusive and unattainable.

If someone progressed, would we even know or recognize the signs of maturation in Christlikeness? Do we have eyes for the milestones, qualities, and activities that mark a maturing follower of Christ?

You may have seen or heard about the Christians who "play the game" or "fake it until they make it." They do Christian things but remain wholly unchanged without progress. Can we for sure say that someone has progressed in their faith? Or is it all guesswork and a gamble?

Undoubtedly, these are real questions and concerns many Christians have thought about and raised question to. However, we can most

With confidence, we can hold up the Ebenezer of another's life and say, "Thus far the Lord has brought them!"

definitely look upon a Christ follower, recognize progress, and affirm their maturation without hesitation. We can have certainty about these matters without labeling them as "arrived." Instead of striving after wind, we can firmly hold onto the real rock in our hands to say progress has been made in their spiritual maturity.

PITFALLS TO AVOID

One of the primary temptations for a group leader is to ***assume*** all the group members understand what you do . . . theologically, scripturally, practically, vocabulary, politically, emotionally, intellectually, etc.

When the group leader makes ***assumptions*** about the group members without exploring where they are in their spiritual maturity, it is like running through a forest blindfolded in the middle of the night. It's dangerous. The group leader could unknowingly run into something at any given time that hurts trust and credibility amongst the group.

Assuming = Uncommunicated Expectations.

Examples of these Pitfalls:

Everyone . . .

"... has the same political views."

"... has a similar level of spiritual maturity."

"... knows my heart."

"... knows Christianese vocabulary."

"... has a salvation testimony they can share."

Assume nothing about everything with everybody.

Instead, think this way:

Everyone . . .

"... has differing political views."

"... has differing levels of spiritual maturity."

"... doesn't know my heart."

"... needs to hear non-Christian vocabulary."

"... has a life story they can share."

HABITS FOR SPIRITUAL GROWTH

DISCIPLES OF JESUS GROW IN . . .

	INDIVIDUALLY "Personally"	**CORPORATELY** "Together"
FELLOWSHIP	Relationship, Prayer, Confess, Belief, Sing, Silence, Reflect	Submit to a Local Church, Participate in Worship Gatherings, Sing
GROW	Read Bible, Meditate, Generosity, Fast, Repent, Rest	Gather with a group
SERVE	At Home, Work, Local Community, "One Another"	With the Body through a Ministry
MULTIPLY	Share the Gospel, Make Disciples	Pray for & Support Global & Local Missions

Listed above is a categorized break down of spiritually formative practices for every disciple of Jesus to pursue and enjoy. Nearly every spiritual practice listed above is a command found in the New Testament.

It is important to realize that you are not what you've done nor what you do. However, what you do determines who you will become. What you practice now shapes you into what you will become.

GROWING THROUGH THE STUDY

LEADING THE STUDY

As the group leader, you are responsible for helping lead and facilitate the study. How you model the study will directly influence your group members' method of personal bible study. Here are some tips to leading discussion:

- Speak 30% and allow discussion for 70%.
- Select a passage, Study ahead of time.
- Learn the historical background.
- Search and Examine the passage.
- Identify the main principle.
- Hit the heart.
- Apply the principle with "What are you going to do with this truth?"

BIBLE STUDY METHODS

Here are some effective methods to studying the bible together:

- Discovery Bible Study
- S.O.A.P.
- The 4 R's (Read, Reflect, Respond, Rest)[4]
- Observation, Interpretation, Application

These are merely a few of many. Learn more about these methods at buildgroups.net/studymethods.

4 Navigators

PHRASES THEY MIGHT SAY

There are *phrases people say* that help identify where they may be at the Table.

LOST	1. "I believe there are many ways to heaven." 2. "I'm a good person." 3. "I think there may be a higher power." 4. "I'm too busy to go to church."
INFANT	1. "Christians are hypocrites." 2. "A loving God would never send me to hell." 3. "The church just wants my money." 4. "I'm too busy to be in a group."
CHILD	1. "I love my church because I feel like I belong." 2. "My group is great! They make me feel at home." 3. "Why do we need to split our group?"
YOUNG ADULT	1. "I'll pass on the movies to visit Bob at the hospital." 2. "I'll serve in kids so parents can worship." 3. "We need to find someone to lead our group that needs to multiply."
PARENT	1. "I'm taking Steve with me next time I visit Bob in the hospital to help him learn how to minister to others." 2. "There are a few *potential leaders* in my group." 3. "I am going to ask Tim to start a new group."[5]

These phrases are not an absolute measurement of another's spiritual maturity but can help evaluate.

5 Diagram – "Phrases They Might Say" – Discipleshift by Putman and Harrington

SELF-IDENTIFYING SPIRITUAL MATURITY

As group leaders, our goal is not to identify and tell others where they are spiritually. Instead, our goal is to identify and help others self-discover what their next step spiritually may be.

How can we help others self-discover?

1. Discovery over informing.
2. Allow the Holy Spirit to be the group's primary discipler.
3. Allow failure for learning opportunities.
4. Lead by example, demonstrate gospel living.
5. Discipleship is more caught than taught.
6. Ask questions in group discussion: "Where do you feel you need to grow? What's your next step spiritually right now?"
7. Challenge them with personal affirmation of progress or potential you see in their life.

The Holy Spirit is your group's primary discipler, not you.

"You who are spiritual should restore him in a spirit of gentleness."

– **GALATIANS 6:1**

HOW WE ARE TO RESPOND

Once we ***discern*** someone's level of spiritual maturity, we must be very cautious to faithfully steward our conclusions.

It is one matter to identify spiritual habits that are missing from a person's life. However, it is another to see the hurtful mess someone's spiritual immaturity and sin can produce.

When we identify their spiritual deficiencies, moving from paper to practice isn't as simple. Emotionally, how we respond can become complex.

For example, when you recognize the group member belittling and cutting off their spouse during the group discussion. Or, when you have the broken and distraught wife sharing about her husband's addiction to porn. The mother who complains incessantly about her children and yells unnecessarily at them. Weekly, they attend under the influence of some substance that causes disruption during the group gathering.

It is very easy to respond in anger, frustration, impatience, and brashness to these situations. We desire justice, righteousness, and restoration. Undoubtedly, it is heart-wrenching to watch a group member, a Christian, to be more hurtful than helpful.

When we move from the ideal to real life, it can become a bit more complicated than what we realize. Hence, it is best to explore how you will respond now as opposed to in the middle of the mess.

There are many ways we can respond:

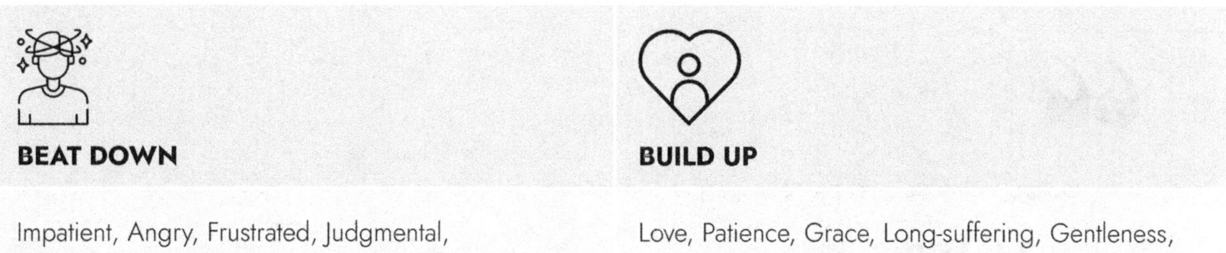

BEAT DOWN	**BUILD UP**
Impatient, Angry, Frustrated, Judgmental, Condescending, Defensive, Careless.	Love, Patience, Grace, Long-suffering, Gentleness, Accepting, Humbly, Considerately.

These are the major ways we can respond for the good or the bad.

It's always easy to discuss this theoretically. However, it's a completely different story to "build up" a husband in your group who treats his wife like trash, and not beat him down instead.

With the tools and information provided in this training, you wield much power that must be used carefully and cautiously. You can use them to be like Anakin Skywalker (villain) or Luke Skywalker (hero). Both possessed great gifting, ability, and power, but chose to use them differently. One for ***destruction***, the other for ***deliverance***.

Use these tools and knowledge for ***building up*** not ***beating down***.

We must do so Biblically in love, patience, and gentleness.

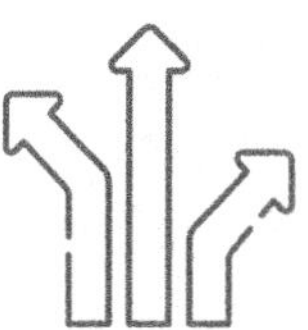

The difference between a hero and bully is simply how they use the same information, power, and ability they both possess – for building up or beating down.

GENTLENESS OVER BRASHNESS

"walk . . . with all humility and gentleness, with patience, bearing with one another in love."

– **EPHESIANS 4:2**

"Gospel comforts must precede gospel corrections"

– **- J.J. SEID**

There are a thousand different messy scenarios you could prepare yourself for with a thousand different best practices. How overwhelming! Mastering a thousand best practices is beyond impractical and unnecessary for a group leader.

You don't need to memorize or have a play book for a thousand different scenarios in group. Let me encourage you with this. If you have love, patience, and gentleness, we will figure it out together. Love patience, and gentleness is all you need, and we will figure out the rest together. Find comfort in that.

Build Leaders. Build Groups. Build Disciples.

GROUP LEADER TRAINING #3

FINAL THOUGHTS

01. A word of caution. Be careful using "The Table of Spiritual Maturity" as the absolute means of determining another's or even your own level of spiritual maturity. It is a linear process that is helpful in part, but not an inspired inerrant system to abide by. "The Table" is linear and helpful in areas, but disciples are far too complex of beings to put into a box. There are immeasurable spiritual qualities "The Table" is unable to measure that cannot be discounted. It's a great way to measure activity in a disciple's life to be on a good trajectory for growth into greater Christlikeness.

02. Don't *tell* others where they are in their spiritual maturity. Instead, help them discover for themselves where they have more to grow by *asking questions or affirming them.*

03. Helping others grow spiritually is one of the most satisfying works to partake in. Do not use these tools and knowledge to abuse but affirm, not beat down but build up, to love not to lash out.

FEEDBACK

What did you think of this training/chapter?

Please take 60 seconds or less to help us make the Group Leader Training better!

We will actually use it to make this training even better!

www.buildgroups.net/glt3feedback

GROUP LEADER TRAINING

SERVE

04

OBJECTIVES

Answer these questions: What is Christlike service? Why does serving matter? As a group leader, how do we mobilize group members to start serving? What does serving do to us?

SCRIPTURE READING

John 13:1-35

TRAINING #4 CHECKLIST

- o Video
- o Fill-in-the-Blanks
- o Essential Belief Assessment
- o Group Discussion
- o Read Chapter 4

CHECKLIST 01

VIDEO

Instructions

Prior to reading the following chapter and attending your next training . . .

Go to www.buildgroups.net/glt4

. . . login, watch the video, and fill-in-the-blanks.

//////////////////////////////

CHECKLIST 02

FILL IN THE BLANKS

Biblical Foundations of "Serve"

How can you, as a group leader, mobilize your group members to begin serving?

– JOHN 13:1-36

1. Jesus stooped down to wash the disciples' feet, which was a _________ job at best

2. Jesus gives the disciple the _______ _________

3. "All people will know you are my disciples by how you ________ one another."

4. The goal of group is that there is a ________ of one another.

5. One of the biggest opportunities you have as a group leader is to sit knee to knee with a group member and say, "___ _____ _______ ___ ______."

6. As the group leader you get to ________ someone and ________ into their life because of your relationship with them.

7. You are ___________ placed to speak this into your group members' lives.

8. Serving is a step of ___________.

9. We Grow ______ service, ____ service, and _________ service

10. You will __________ things you otherwise wouldn't by serving and getting skin in the game.

11. Get the bus __________ and then we can steer someone into the proper place of service God is calling them to.

12. The most important thing you can do as a group leader is get them ________ into service.

13. Don't let your group members miss out on the _________ of serving Jesus.

14. Moving from the ____________ to the ____________ stage is thrilling.

15. When you get to be a ________ in helping build that Kingdom and seeing God work, it's at those ___________ you will experience some of the most fun, exhilarating, and _______________ moments in the Christian life.

16. Wash feet, serve people, and love them, that is how people will know you are a ___________ of Jesus Christ.

CHECKLIST 03

ESSENTIAL BELIEF ASSESSMENT

Purpose

To expose and give people the opportunity to explore the essential beliefs or doctrines of the Christian faith. This is not a pass or fail exam; but, rather, it is a chance to learn important Biblical beliefs together.

		True	False	Unsure
01	The Bible is the highest authority for what I believe.	☐	☐	☐
02	The purpose of the Christian Life is to become the best version of self possible.	☐	☐	☐
03	It is very important to me personally to encourage non-Christians to trust Jesus Christ as their Savior.	☐	☐	☐
04	The Bible's condemnation of homosexual behavior doesn't apply today.	☐	☐	☐
05	Since Christ has paid the debt of sin, it is permissible to continue intentional sinful practices.	☐	☐	☐
06	If I do not follow the commands of Christ, I will lose my salvation.	☐	☐	☐
07	It pleases God to punish his children for their disobedience.	☐	☐	☐
08	The Great Commission is to evangelize the world with the gospel of Jesus Christ.	☐	☐	☐
09	Sex outside of traditional marriage is a sin.	☐	☐	☐
10	Modern science disproves the Bible.	☐	☐	☐

Refer to this link for the answer guide: https://www.buildgroups.net/eba4

CHECKLIST 04

GROUP DISCUSSION

1. What were your thoughts on the video?
2. Quick Hitter Question: In 60 seconds or less, share about the first area you began serving in or through the local church and how you ended up serving there.
3. What's something you learned from serving in a ministry?
4. How can we help others start serving?
5. What are obstacles that prevent or keep people from serving?
6. How can we help people overcome these obstacles? What are some solutions?
7. How can group service projects help group members to start serving?

CHECKLIST 05

SERVE

BIBLICAL FOUNDATIONS

SELFISH TO SERVICE

We all ***serve*** in some way in our lives.

The problem is that we almost always tend to primarily ***serve self.***

Everything in the world screams to do the ***opposite*** of what Jesus did.

Jesus should have . . .

01	Fought Back.
02	Not Surrendered.
03	Protested for Rights.
04	Looked Out for #1 (Self).

Jesus calls us to a life of ***service*** and ***sacrifice:***

1. Jesus Washes the Disciples' Feet – John 13:1-5
2. "They were selling their possessions distributing to all who had need" – Acts 2:45
3. "***Serve one another*** humbly in love" – Galatians 5:13

We grow in selflessness by being *less* about *me.*

"Count others as more significant than yourself."

– **PHILIPPIANS 2:3**

JOY is a way to remember ***God's priorities*** for my life:

- Jesus
- Others
- You

WHY SERVE

We serve for several reasons. Serving is discipleship. Serving grows us. Disciples grow into greater Christlikeness through serving. There are three important parts and purposes to serving that mature us as Christ followers:

Disciples of Jesus . . .

01	Grow FOR service.
02	Grow IN service.
03	Grow FROM service.

Since service is essential to make spiritually formed disciples of Jesus Christ, our first goal in this chapter is to ***help you, help others*** to discover their ***Ministry Arena***.

A *Ministry Arena* is the spiritual battlefield that God calls a person to. God has uniquely wired, gifted, and imbued his children with certain talents. Truly, these gifts and abilities are provided so that his children will use them to fulfill the Great Commission.

"Now there are varieties of gifts, but the same Spirit . . . and there are varieties of activities, but the same God who empowers them all in everyone. To each is given the manifestation of the Spirit for the common good."

– **1 CORINTHIANS 12:4-7**

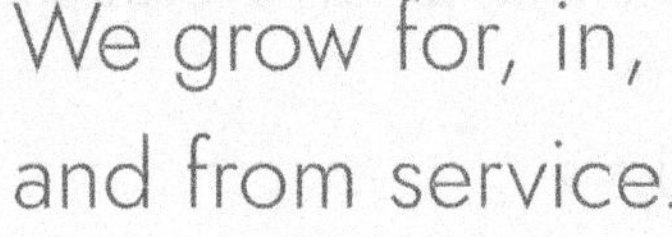

We grow for, in, and from service.

Everyone has a ministry arena that God calls them to with the intention of using their gifts and abilities to receive the blessing of contributing to the Kingdom.

When someone discovers their ministry arena, which can and does change from season to season, it will significantly increase their trajectory for greater Christlikeness.

Our second goal is to ***help you, help others*** to grow in their serving.

As people grow in their service, they are transformed more into the image of Christ.

As people begin serving, it activates a deeper passion for ownership of their faith and relationship with God

HOW TO HELP OTHERS SERVE

GET THE BUS MOVING

When helping others to begin serving, the best rule of thumb is to just *get the bus moving*.

Most people don't begin serving because they're ***indecisive:***

1. What's my Ministry Arena?
2. What are my Spiritual Gifts?
3. What are my Passions?
4. Will I really enjoy serving there?

Discovering one's ministry arena is a time to **do** and **pray**.

People don't begin serving because they ***over-spiritualize*** the ***process***. These are good questions to ask, but not to get stuck on:

1. Pray about it?
2. Do I have Peace?
3. Wait on the Lord?
4. Wait? Be? Or . . . .

Discovering one's ministry arena is not a time to ***wait*** and ***be*** but ***do*** and ***pray.***

The best way for people to discover their ministry arena is by ***test driving***. A test drive is allowing a potential new volunteer to try out serving in a specific ministry a few times and give feedback to their experience (liked or disliked) with no strings attached. It's a safe way for a person to explore a call to a specific ministry. Here are a few benefits:

1. Low Risk.
2. Removes fear of commitment.
3. Removes fear of disappointing others.
4. No opportunity to disappoint themselves.

Activity helps to ***steer*** the ***bus*** into the right ministry arena. ***Inactivity*** makes it ***impossible*** to ***steer*** the ***bus*** into the right ministry arena for the individual.

You must move the bus before you can steer the bus.

HELPING OTHERS GROW "IN" SERVING

STAGES OF SERVING

As a group leader, you can look for ways to help people ***advance*** in their ministry arena.

Everyone starts at a different stage of serving. Some begin at a walk, others a jog, and some a run.

Walk		Low-hanging fruit.
Jog	=	Medium-hanging fruit.
Run		High-hanging fruit.

It's helpful to keep in mind that most people start at a walk. We must demonstrate ***faithfulness*** in the ***little*** things before we are entrusted with the ***big*** things.[6]

On the following page, there is a visual example of where disciples can discover their ministry arena and potentially grow in that area with greater responsibility.

6 Luke 16:10

HELPING OTHERS GROW "IN" SERVING

[OUTWARD]

MINISTRY ARENA	WALK	JOG	RUN
Connections	Bulletins, Parking Lot, Door Greeter	Guest Services	Team Lead
Hospitality	Coffee Bar, Meal Train Participant	Meal Train Coordinator	Host a Group
Groups	Co-Leader	Group Leader	Groups Coach
Students	Volunteer	Group Co-Leader	Group Leader, Coach
Kids	Helper	Teacher	Team Lead
Worship Band	Band Practice Team	Band Worship Gatherings	Worship Leader
Media	Volunteer	Team Lead	Director
Safety	Security Guard, Medical	Team Lead	Director
Care	Write Letters	Call Members	Hospital Visits

Now, increased responsibility does not always equate to spiritual growth for the individual. If this were the case, then only those gifted with leadership would be considered spiritually mature. However, that's just not the case Biblically. The body is made up of many parts. Demonstrating a gift of leadership is not the ultimate show of maturity. It is merely one manifestation of the Spirit working through a part of the body. More activity and responsibility do not always necessitate spiritual growth or maturity. In many ways, it does, but not in every case. For example, a person may start and stay serving as a greeter forever. Therefore, the chart below shows in what ways a person can grow ***from*** serving in a ministry arena. The former measures activity and responsibility, while, on the inside, this measures the inward growth and transformation of the person dedicated to an area of service over time.

GROWING "FROM" SERVICE

[INWARD]

SIT	WALK	JOG	RUN
"Ought To"	"Want To"	"Get To"	"Must Do"
A Duty to Serve	A Desire to Serve	A Blessing to Serve	A Passion to Serve
Unmoved To	Likes To	Privileged To	Thirsts To
Duty Bound	Partial Duty & Delight	Delight	Deep Delight

As seen in the figure, "Growing 'From' Service", there is also an immeasurable side of a disciple growing in their service. Not only can the disciple grow outwardly in their ministry responsibilities to more influence and leadership, the disciple also grows inwardly as a result of their serving. Despite the size of ministry responsibility, impact, or influence, the disciple can grow in their Christlikeness inwardly. In fact, the disciple can remain serving in a smaller ministry influence with less quantitative people affected, but at the same time, they can still be spiritually formed into the image of Christ inwardly and have their hearts shaped into the desires of Christ's.

Despite the size of one's ministry responsibility, impact, or influence, the disciple grows inwardly from their serving.

GROUP SERVICE PROJECTS

SERVING TOGETHER

Some people may be hesitant about serving in just a ***walk*** option. Moving from "sitting" to "walking" can be a big, scary step for many people.

Our goal is to meet people where they are the way Jesus did and help them take the next step.

A great way to help people take their next step into the "walk" serving stage may be through a ***group service project***.

Group Service Projects are one of the most effective ways to mobilize group members to begin serving.

Serving alongside others . . . .

1. . . . they ***know*** makes people more ***comfortable*** and ***confident*** in their serving.
2. . . . strengthens and deepens the group's ***relationships.***
3. . . . gives an opportunity to practice ***gifts.***
4. . . . provides opportunity to ***discover desires*** people have for specific areas of service.

Here are some Group Service Project Examples:

1. Paint a home.
2. Neighborhood cleanup.
3. Write a letter to missionaries.
4. Host a neighborhood grill out for outreach.
5. Host a season holiday party (Halloween, New Years, etc.) for outreach to others.
6. Yardwork for a friend or neighbor (rake leaves, bag leaves, mow, trim, etc.) in neighborhood.
7. Volunteer for VBS or some other annual church ministry event.
8. Host an outreach dinner to witness to an unbeliever together as a group.
9. Volunteer at the local community foodbank.

Build Leaders. Build Groups. Build Disciples.

GROUP LEADER TRAINING #4

FINAL THOUGHTS

01. Invite people into the thrill of serving God to receive the blessing of being a blessing.

02. We don't use people for ministry, people are the ministry.

03. We want to equip people and affirm them into the ministry God is calling them to, not the ministry we have the greatest need in.

04. Get the bus moving so they can begin growing *for, in,* and *from* their service to God and others.

05. Don't devalue another's *inward* growth *"from"* serving if they do not grow *"in"* their service outwardly to a leadership level. Value those who start and stay for a lifetime in one ministry role. Value every member of the body as it builds itself up in love.

FEEDBACK

What did you think of this training/chapter?

Please take 60 seconds or less to help us make the Group Leader Training better!

We will actually use it to make this training even better!

www.buildgroups.net/glt4feedback

GROUP LEADER TRAINING

MULTIPLY

OBJECTIVES

Answer these questions: What does it mean to multiply a group? What is the end goal of a group? How can a group multiply? Is group for unbelievers? How can a group be evangelistic?

SCRIPTURE READING

Matthew 28:16-20; Acts 6:1, 9:31, 12:24; 2 Timothy 2:2

TRAINING #5 CHECKLIST

- o Video
- o Fill-in-the-Blanks
- o Essential Belief Assessment
- o Group Discussion
- o Read Chapter 5

CHECKLIST 01

VIDEO

Instructions

Prior to reading the following chapter and attending your next training . . .

Go to www.buildgroups.net/glt5

. . . login, watch the video, and fill-in-the-blanks.

//////////////////////////////

CHECKLIST 02

FILL IN THE BLANKS

Biblical Foundations of "MULTIPLY"

Read Matthew 28:16-20

1. The ________ _________ is what Jesus gives to his disciples present an all disciples to come.

2. The Great Commission is __________ the Great Commands into Christ's disciples.

Read Acts 1:8

3. Three impossible tasks that Jesus gives his disciples:
    1. ______________________________
    2. ______________________________
    3. ______________________________

4. In Matthew 28:16-20, Jesus calls his disciples up to a ________ _____ where he gives them what's called the _________ ____________

5. In Acts 1:8, there are no disciples ________.

6. As we look at this idea of multiplying a group and the Kingdom, it can be done by ________ your group to start a new one or to ______ your _______ with unbelievers.

7. The best way to share your faith is to do it in ___________ with other believers.

8. As you are pursuing the Great Commission to multiply the Great Commands into Christ's disciples, remember, Jesus is _______ you always to the end of the ages.

CHECKLIST 03

ESSENTIAL BELIEF ASSESSMENT

Purpose

To expose and give people the opportunity to explore the essential beliefs or doctrines of the Christian faith. This is not a pass or fail exam; but, rather, it is a chance to learn important Biblical beliefs together.

		True	False	Unsure
01	The Bible is outdated and could use a few updates to be more useful for today.	☐	☐	☐
02	God is Triune in nature, which is like H2O having three parts: liquid water, ice, or evaporated fog.	☐	☐	☐
03	For spiritual formation to happen in a person, they only need the God's Spirit and God's Word.	☐	☐	☐
04	All sins are equal in severity.	☐	☐	☐
05	The Holy Spirit is the person of the Trinity who breathes life into humanity.	☐	☐	☐
06	The word of God is living and active.	☐	☐	☐
07	The purpose of the Christian life is to become more like Christ in his character and nature.	☐	☐	☐
08	The Great Commission is Evangelism and Discipleship.	☐	☐	☐
09	A relationship with God is personal and private.	☐	☐	☐
10	When God speaks, his word almost always comes true.	☐	☐	☐

Refer to this link for the answer guide: https://www.buildgroups.net/eba5

CHECKLIST 04

GROUP DISCUSSION

1. What were your thoughts on the video?

2. Icebreaker: You have to sing karaoke. What song do you pick?

3. Quick Hitter Question: In 60 seconds or less, what is the purpose of the group?

4. What is the end goal of the group?

5. Why do groups multiply (start a new group out of the existing group)? How is it a blessing?

6. Think of a time you wanted to or did share the gospel with someone.
   How did it go? What were your feelings?

7. What are your biggest roadblocks to sharing the gospel with other people?

8. What are highways to sharing the gospel more?

9. Can group be an avenue for unbelievers to join?

CHECKLIST 04

MULTIPLY

BIBLICAL FOUNDATIONS

MULTIPLY WHAT MATTERS

We all ***multiply*** something in our lives. Some multiply children, others multiply money, another multiplies their network. As disciples of Christ, we are to multiply disciples.

"Go therefore and make disciples of all nations, baptizing them in the name of the Father, Son, and Holy Spirit, teaching them to observe all that I have commanded you."

– **MATTHEW 28:19-20**

Jesus ***entrusts*** us with the Great Commission. We are invited in by Jesus to help fulfill the Great Commission.

The Great Commission tasks us to multiply the Great Commands into Christ's disciples.

The outcome of fulfilling the Great Commission results in disciples of Christ who *love God* and *love people.*

Is the Great Commission solely about missions and evangelism? No.

One is not more important than the other. Evangelism and Discipleship are equally important and to both be pursued, practiced, and observed.

The Great Commission is Evangelism and Discipleship.

However, ***making disciples*** is a frightening endeavor for most people. There are many legitimate fears Christ followers face in not just sharing the gospel, but, also in raising others up spiritually in the faith.

When the disciples were tasked with the Great Commission, they also feared and doubted how they were to accomplish such a feat.

Jesus perceives their ***doubt,*** then ***comforts*** and ***encourages*** his disciples by saying, "All authority in heaven and on earth has been given to me . . . I am with you always, until the end of the ages."

Jesus ***challenges*** and ***walks*** with us to ***build us up*** to accomplish the mission he's entrusted us to fulfill.

We are called to spread the Gospel by ***making disciples,*** not ***make converts*** by spreading the Gospel.

As we ***make*** and ***mature*** gospel driven disciples who love God and love people, we will intentionally move towards ***sharing the Gospel*** with the ***unbelieving***.

Remember, sharing the Gospel with the unbelieving takes ***time***, ***investment, encouragement,*** and an ***example*** set for one another.

END GOALS OF GROUP

HIT THE MARK

There are several desirable biblical outcomes that we see the New Testament Church live out. As groups gather in homes, their spiritual practices bring about several end goals we can strive for today.

Here are some New Testament end goals of group:

1. Share the Gospel with others outside the group.
2. Invite other people into the group to hear the Gospel.
3. Invite unconnected people into the group.
4. New leaders are discovered in your group.
5. Multiply by sending out new leaders to start a new group.

In the New Testament, groups never existed to clam up or close down into the holy huddle. Rather, as unbelievers witnessed the attractional community of the New Testament Church through home groups connecting, growing, and serving together, "the Lord added to their number day by day those who were being saved."[7]

As groups Fellowship, Grow, and Serve together well, the Lord Multiplies groups by adding more who believe.

The life-giving transformational practice of New Testament groups proclaimed the excellencies of God with their lives.

"But you are a chosen race, a royal priesthood, a holy nation, a people for his own possession, that you may proclaim the excellencies of him who called you out of darkness into his marvelous light."

– **1 PETER 2:9**

Biblically, the end goal of groups is to multiply.

7 Acts 2:47

THE BLESSINGS OF "MULTIPLYING"

BENEFITS AND BLESSINGS

What are the blessings and benefits of multiplying your group?

Initially, it can be a little nerve racking for some to consider multiplying their group to start a new one.

It can hurt to say goodbye to someone you do life with in your group and have a close relationship with. Undoubtedly, it is a real feeling to miss someone who could potentially leave your group and therefore lose some community with them. However, there are so many blessings to multiplying.

Here are some blessings to multiplying your group:

1. Room is made for people who aren't here yet.
2. The Gospel advances to more people.
3. The Kingdom of God expands farther.
4. Opportunity is available for another to possibly lead.
5. We get to do ministry like Jesus did.
6. We get to practice sending people out to make disciples locally, nationally, or possibly even globally.
7. We help provide others an opportunity to exercise their gifts.
8. Multiplying helps move people around "The Table of Spiritual Maturity".
9. Multiplying helps us become more selfless and "others" focused.
10. Multiplying is some of the most fertile soil for individual growth and sanctification.

What if I told you the next lead pastor of your church was in your group?
What if I told you multiplying your group made room for the person who would become the next missionary sent out of your church?

What if I told you neither have been called to this ministry yet, but they will discover this when they join your group and eventually are given the opportunity to lead their own group.

Your group multiplying may be the first domino to all of this.

Multiplication is powerful!

HELPING OTHERS SHARE THE GOSPEL

ROADBLOCKS TO SHARING THE GOSPEL

There are many reasons why people do not share the gospel. Some reasons are legitimate while others . . . maybe not so much. However, as a group leader and shepherd over someone's life, we must be longsuffering and meet them where they are to lovingly guide them into greater Christlikeness.

Here are some possible reasons why people don't share the gospel:

1. Afraid of what people will think.
2. Unsure they will know what to say.
3. Uncertain if they can answer people's questions.
4. Don't encounter unbelievers very often.
5. Feel inadequate to share the gospel.
6. Don't fully know how to communicate the gospel.
7. Makes them very uncomfortable.
8. Worried they'll be awkward.
9. They don't feel like an expert.

Many of these are real concerns for the everyday Christian. As a group leader, there are ways that we can help build people's confidence and equip them to share the gospel with other people.

HIGHWAYS TO SHARING THE GOSPEL

To help others share the gospel, you need to identify their roadblocks or concerns, and then also gracefully speak truth into the situation.

Here are some truths to speak into their lives with grace and gentleness:

1. You don't have to be an expert.
2. Only God saves. It's not your responsibility for the person to receive the gospel.
3. We are called to share the message, not have the unbeliever receive it.
4. God saves people through awkwardness.
5. Discomfort is a great way to learn to share the gospel better with more confidence.
6. Discomfort helps grow you and excites us into the faith even more.

7. Be intentional about getting around unbelievers with spare time.
8. Pray God would bring unbelievers into your path to share the gospel with; you'll be surprised to see what happens.
9. Everyone is a missionary to spread the gospel locally and globally.

HOW GROUPS ADVANCE THE GOSPEL

As a group leader, what can you do with and through your group to share the gospel more? What are some practices, avenues, opportunities, studies, prayers, or even questions that can be asked to help your group share the gospel more?

Here are some examples of how your group can advance the gospel:

1. Group outreach night, where everyone invites their co-workers, friends, or neighbors for a hang out to build relationships with them.
2. Encourage one another to share the gospel.
3. Pray for one another to share the gospel.
4. Pray for the salvation of unbelievers by name.
5. Point out the mission field or opportunities to one another.
6. Follow up to ask if a group member had the chance to share the gospel with a person they said or prayed for by name.
7. Group service projects in the local community and in your neighborhoods can build an ongoing relationship for a gospel witness.
8. Ask questions that focus the group on sharing the gospel like, "Whose salvation are you praying for right now?"
9. Take turns sharing life stories or salvation testimonies (if all have one) in the group gathering

There are many ways that a group can advance the gospel together without being theological gospel experts who preach like Billy Graham.

However, number nine is one of the most effective ways for group members to start sharing the gospel more. Why? No one can justifiably get upset with your life story or salvation testimony because it's your experience. The fear of rejection is removed. Practice sharing life stories in the group gathering and it will inevitably train group members to share with others.

Advancing and sharing the Gospel is always better done together.

GROUP . . . FOR UNBELIEVERS?

SHOULD UNBELIEVERS BE IN OUR GROUP?

Every church and groups ministry have a different approach to fulfill the purpose of their groups. Some purpose groups to serve as closed gatherings of accountability. Others are open to connect as many people as possible to a group. Another is designed specifically to share the gospel with missional living. At the end of the day, it is most important that you submit and champion the vision and purpose of groups your church communicates and encourages. Nonetheless, if you are considering having an unbeliever join or belong in your group, here are some great resources to use as an aid.

Can your group be an avenue for ***unbelievers*** to join and belong?

It is good to allow unbelievers to come into your group under the right circumstances. Allowing an unbeliever to visit or join your group can really engage the group together in conversation. On the other hand, an unbeliever in the group can minimize the spiritual depth your group can build towards. There's only so far an unbeliever can go with the entire group into deeper spiritual matters. However, it doesn't mean that an unbeliever cannot join, attend, and benefit from a group.

When it comes to considering unbelievers joining your group, it is not a wholesale yes or no. Allowing unbelievers to join your group must be a case-by-case scenario because no two persons are alike, and no two groups are alike. As the group leader, you must protect the group from an unbeliever that could cause damage to the community. At the same time, you must provide opportunity for the group to be stretched to be a gospel witness to unbelievers. Jesus often refused to give a foothold or platform for his enemies to speak into matters with his disciples[8]. Yet, Jesus constantly had his disciples around sinners. Enemies and sinners are different groups of people in the New Testament. While Jesus was amongst the sinners, Jesus kept his enemies at a distance for the most part.

Allowing an unbeliever to join your group is right and wrong.

8 Mark 1:25

There are different types of unbelievers in the world that could join your group. Sometimes it is right for you to let them join. Other times it is wrong. Inviting an unbeliever into your group is a matter of discernment.

Here are some simple questions to ask before allowing an unbeliever to join your group:

1. Is this unbeliever truly seeking spiritual things?
2. Or, are they seeking to be a disruption?
3. Is this unbeliever respectful or disrespectful in their interactions and conversation with believers?
4. Is this unbeliever tolerant of Christian views even though they might disagree?
5. Is this unbeliever seeking to have enriching conversations or to cause division and chaos amongst the group?
6. Is the unbeliever genuinely interested in what the group has to share, or are they dismissive and unwilling to engage in the conversation?
7. Is the unbeliever trustworthy to keep important matters of the group confidential or would they weaponize it for intentional slander or gossip?

Build Leaders. Build Groups. Build Disciples.

GROUP LEADER TRAINING #5

FINAL THOUGHTS

01. Biblically, the end goal of groups is to multiply.

02. There are far more blessings to multiplying than disadvantages.

03. Sharing the Gospel is always done best together.

04. It's right for unbelievers to join your group, but not always.

05. Help your group share the gospel by removing the roadblocks and getting them on the highway.

FEEDBACK

What did you think of this training/chapter?

Please take 60 seconds or less to help us make the Group Leader Training better!

We will actually use it to make this training even better!

www.buildgroups.net/glt5feedback

Build Leaders. Build Groups. Build Disciples.

GROUP LEADER TRAINING COURSE

FINAL THOUGHTS

1. Healthy Groups practice fellowshipping (relationship), growing (transformation), serving (contribution), and multiplying (mission).

2. Healthy groups require healthy leaders with healthy doctrine, healthy expectations, a transformative Gospel, and a local church's support and oversight.

3. Manage your own expectations well of what you can expect from your group. It takes time to train a group into healthiness.

4. The Holy Spirit is the primary discipler for both you ***and*** your group members.

5. Serving is discipleship. We grow for, in, and from serving – mobilize your people to serve so they can grow.

6. Multiplying is the beautiful life stage of a group where group members blossom into what's been poured into them by the group that you made possible by leading.

7. Build Leaders. Build Groups. Build Disciples.

REFERENCES

Since I have been influenced by many books and Christian leaders that pertain to groups, leadership, and church ministry, it is difficult to recall if some of the contents of these book are truly originally mine or not. Nonetheless, I wish to reference, acknowledge, and give credit to many of these Christian leaders and books that impacted me personally. Undoubtedly, these incredible leaders and resources aided in my own ministry execution and formation of the Group Leader Training Course Workbook over the years:

LEADERS

- John Theisen, Midway Church
- Jared Stillings, Heritage Baptist Church
- Jeff Scott, Heritage Baptist Church
- Adam Bowers, First Free Church
- Jared Musgrove, The Village Church
- Matt Moore, Providence Church
- Justin Elafros, The Village Church
- J.J. Seid, Frontline Church
- Chad Sebby, TheForge.org
- Miguel Warren, Lighthouse Church
- Stephen Pollitte, Gateway Community Church

BOOKS

- ***Small Groups with Purpose*** by Steve Gladen
- ***Leading Small Groups with Purpose*** by Steve Gladen
- ***Transformational Groups*** by Stetzer & Geiger
- ***Life Giving Groups*** by Jeremy Linneman
- ***Leading Healthy, Multiplying Small Groups*** by Rod Dempsey & Dave Earley
- **Community** by Brad House
- **The Essential Guide for Small Group Leaders** by Bill Search

- *Leading Small Groups* by Chris Surratt
- *Deep Discipleship* by J.T. English
- *Spiritual Leadership* by J. Oswald Sanders
- *Designed to Lead* by Kevin Peck & Eric Geiger
- *Building Leaders* by Aubrey Malphurs & Will Mancini
- *The Conviction to Lead* by Albert Mohler
- *Spiritual Leadership* by Henry & Richard Blackaby
- *Delighting in the Trinity* by Michael Reeves
- *Caring for One Another* by Ed Welch
- *4 Chair Discipling* by Dann Spader
- *Discipleshift* by Jim Putman & Bobby Harrington
- *Real-Life Discipleship Training Manual* by Jim Putman & Bill Krause
- *Simple Church* by Thom S. Rainer & Eric Geiger
- *Purpose Driven Youth Ministry* by Doug Fields
- *Church Planter* by Darrin Patrick
- *Sticky Leaders* by Larry Osbourne
- *Next Generation Leader* by Andy Stanley

Credit to Midway Church of Pilot Point, TX, and The Village Church, Flower Mound, TX, for whole or partial bits of their statements of faith listed on pages 46-47 in a concise, precise, edifying, and understandable manner.

Please Leave a Book Review on 

Search **"Group Leader Training by Adam Erlichman"** on Amazon

GET THE ENTIRE SERIES

Book 01	What is a Disciple?
Book 02	Heart Posture
Book 03	Look & Love
Book 04	The Essentials
Book 05	What Doing Does

CHURCH NEXT STEP

RESOURCES

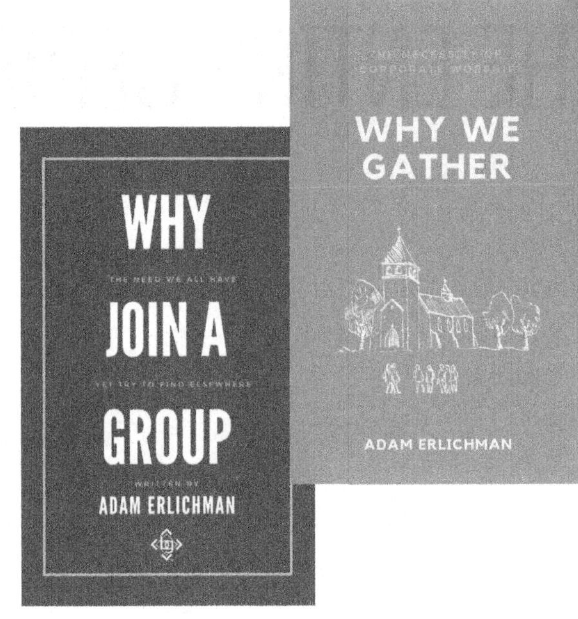

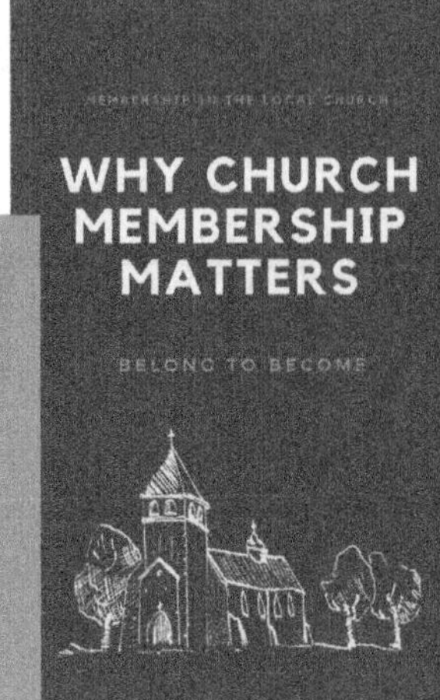

Why Church Membership Matters: ***Belong to Become***

Why We Gather: ***The Necessity of Corporate Worship***

Why Join a Group: ***The Need We All Have Yet Try to Find Elsewhere***

Why We Serve: ***Saved People Serve People***

Why We Study God's Word: ***The Message of Life***

CONNECT WITH

BUILD GROUPS

Build Groups
(Group Leaders & Pastors)
www.buildgroups.net

Trainings

Consulting

Coaching

Cohorts

Books and Resources

BE THE FIRST TO HEAR ABOUT

NEW BOOKS FROM BUILD GROUPS!

Sign up for announcements about new and upcoming titles at: ***BuildGroups.net/signup***

Facebook / Instagram ***@Build_Groups***

Don't miss out on our great reads!

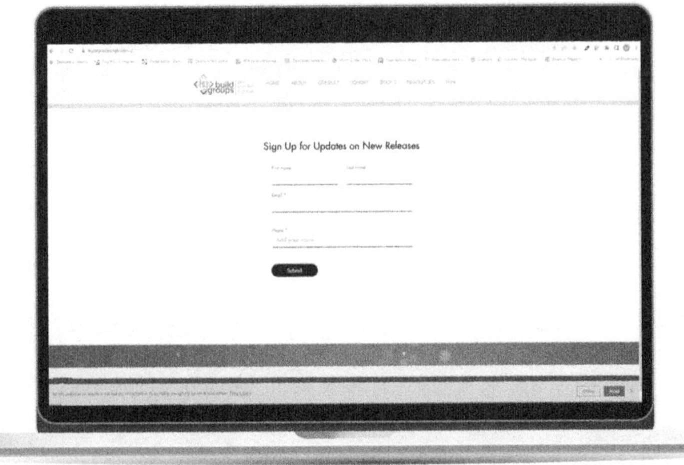

FREE RESOURCES

Download your free resources "For Everyday Christians," Small Group Leaders and more:
www.buildgroups.net/resources

- 5 Essential Belief Assessments
- Spiritual Habits Chart
- Spiritual Growth Assessment
- Baptism Brochure
- Why Church Membership Matters
- Regular Blogs – ***www.buildgroups.net/blog***

CONNECT WITH PASTOR/AUTHOR

ADAM ERLICHMAN

Speaking | Consulting | Books and Resources
www.buildgroups.net/speaking

Email: ***adam@buildgroups.net***

Facebook / Instagram ***@adam.e.erlichman / @adamerlichman***

Learn how Adam can help your church

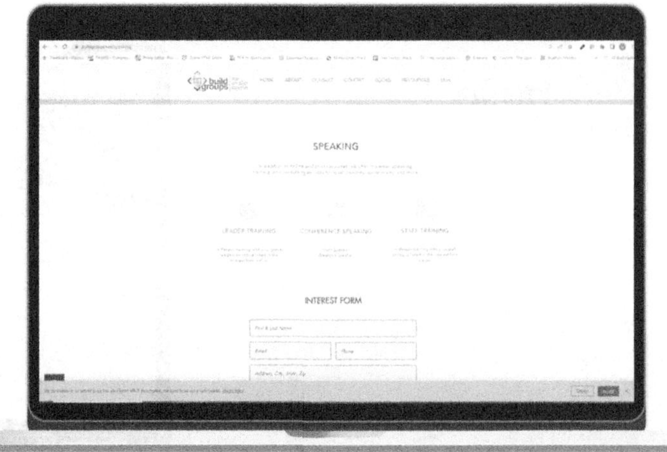

Adam Erlichman is a Pastor, Consultant, and Best-Selling Author with Build Groups, LLC. He has served on various church staffs in Executive, Groups, Discipleship, Young Adult, and Youth ministries. Adam's ministry focuses on Groups, Discipleship, Solving the Volunteer Crisis, Strategic Planning, Family Discipleship, and Leadership Development. He serves on the Southern Baptist Texas Convention (SBTC) Discipleship Team/Board. Adam became a Christian and studied at Liberty University. He is passionate to see every day Christians equipped and mobilized to make and multiply disciples. Stories of life transformation are his addiction.

Made in the USA
Monee, IL
06 August 2025